It Happened In Series

IT HAPPENED ON THE OREGON TRAIL

Tricia Martineau Wagner

TWODOT®

GUILFORD, CONNECTICUT
HELENA, MONTANA

AN IMPRINT OF THE GLOBE PEQUOT PRESS

A · TWODOT® · BOOK

Library of Congress Cataloging-in-Publication Data

Wagner, Tricia Martineau
It happened on the Oregon Trail / Tricia Martineau Wagner. — 1st ed.
p. cm. — (It happened in series)
Includes bibliographical references and index.
ISBN 0-7627-2579-6
1. Oregon National Historic Trail—History—Anecdotes. 2. Frontier and pioneer life—West (U.S.)—Anecdotes. 3. Overland journeys to the Pacific—Anecdotes. 4. West (U.S.)—History—19th century—Anecdotes. 5. West (U.S.)—Biography—Anecdotes. I. Title. II. Series.

F597.W34 2004
978'.02—dc22 2004057998

Manufactured in the United States of America
First Edition/First Printing

In memory of my mother, Merreck E. Martineau,
who said everything beautifully.

Contents

Acknowledgments

We can all be thankful for the courageous pioneers who took time to write in their diaries and journals and who later offered their reminiscences about their cross-country treks over the westward trails. Without their insight into this fascinating period in American history, our understanding of it would be much poorer. The voices of these ordinary people who endured an extraordinary experience teach us that everyone has a story.

This book came to fruition with generous assistance from the following people:

- Those who pointed me in the right direction when I began my research: Kevin Howard, Gordon Howard, Dean Knudsen, and Art Johnson.
- My editors at The Globe Pequot Press, Charlene Patterson, whose expert direction made the editing process simply enjoyable, Erin Turner, who took me to a new level, and Shelley Wolf, whose attention to detail brought the manuscript together.
- Beth Radmall Olsen, for her willingness to share her wealth of knowledge of the Rebecca Winters story, and all the descendants and friends of Rebecca Winters. Likewise I thank William J. Curtis for sharing his research on Emily Fisher.
- For their assistance in uncovering historical documents and newspaper articles, Doris E. Onorato at the Van Allen House Heritage Center in Mt. Pleasant, Iowa, Vickie Clause at the North Platte Valley Historical Association in Gering, Nebraska, and Janice Schultz at the Mid-Continent Public Library in Independence, Missouri.

- Allen Harrison and John Cook from the National Oregon and California Trail Center in Montpelier, Idaho, for information on their museum.
- Wallace deYoung, who figured out the value of a modern dollar in 1850—on Wells Fargo's time.
- For their continual assistance, the staffs at Dublin Public Library (CA) and the San Ramon Public Library (CA), especially Robin Calogne and Steve Ginochio.
- Deidre Bolick, who assisted with the typing.
- Kevin Fitzgerald, for his technical support and expertise, which got me started. Thank you, my friend.
- The value of constant friends cannot be underestimated. Thank you, Sharon DeNicola, Melissa Johnson, Nancy Mills, Joan Rush, and Janet Chi for the kind words.
- My husband and best friend, Mark, who lead me kicking and screaming into the world of computers, which did indeed simplify my life. His love and encouragement made my dream come true.
- Our children, Kelsey Merreck and Mitchell Dale, for listening to all my stories with wide-eyed interest and for sharing in my excitement. Always follow your dreams.

Introduction

No two journeys over the Oregon Trail were the same. For some, the overland trip was a carefree and scenic experience of a lifetime. Unencumbered by accident, disease, or misfortune, theirs was an adventure-filled, if not a romantic, affair. For others, the cross-country trek was nothing short of grueling, with unexpected hardships and unbearable heartaches. They experienced intolerable extremes of weather; lacked the basic necessities of food, water, and shelter; and witnessed inconceivable human behavior.

When the wagon train era began in the 1840s, thousands of courageous emigrants left behind the America they knew and traveled into uncharted territory across unfamiliar terrain—at times unsure of the route, let alone what to expect ahead. West of the Missouri River towns was a wild frontier as foreign to them as living in a space station seems to us today.

The flood tide of emigrants over westward trails began as a trickle and evolved into a tidal wave that left the Native Americans overwhelmed by the sheer volume of trespassers. Caught up in the "Oregon Fever," the emigrants were collectively driven toward fresh horizons, and thus the caravans of wagons began rolling westward. Perhaps it was the chance for a better life, free land, the hope to strike it rich, the desire to unite the land as one nation, or simply an adventuresome spirit that led them to leave behind their lives in the eastern United States. In the span of forty-five short years, the United States went from being a country made up of towns east of the Mississippi River to a nation that stretched from sea to shining sea.

There are several myths about the settlement of the West that need to be dispelled to gain a clear understanding of this time in American history. The first myth is that the Oregon Trail was one long, continuous road. More accurately it was like a network of blood vessels that trailed westward, gathering into a pulsating vein in the vicinity of Fort Kearney, Nebraska. From there the Oregon Trail headed in a westerly direction with additional cutoffs being defined along the way as the travelers sought the quickest route to the Pacific coast.

The second myth involves the image of a single-file line of wagons heading toward the setting sun. In actuality an array of wagons spread out one abreast of the other, row behind row, to avoid the choking dust. The path a caravan took was often a mile wide, due to the natural detours caused by changes in river courses or the necessity of finding available grass and fresh campsites.

Third is the misconception that men, with their brute strength, tamed the West alone. Largely ignored by historians is the importance that women played in settling and civilizing the wild frontier. The women's strength and courage under adverse conditions saw their families through unfathomable situations.

The fourth myth is that travelers over the Oregon Trail were a homogeneous group of Caucasian American citizens. The Oregon Trail opened its doors to many immigrants who left their homelands for a better life. It was a melting pot of hopefuls with diverse ethnic backgrounds from Europe and around the world. Germans, Poles, Irish, Asians, Greeks, Russians, and African Americans, both slave and free, were among the many who journeyed over the Oregon Trail.

Absorbed into the American psyche is the fifth myth: that travelers over the Oregon Trail were constantly in danger of attack by Indians. In fact, Indian attacks were rare, though cultural ignorance on the part of the emigrants was cause for misunderstandings. While atrocities were committed on both sides, only the attacks by Indians were highly publicized. Though the emigrants were initially given a wide berth by the local tribes, years of conflict between the Indians and the U.S. military strained relations between the two groups. Indians refused to simply give up their land without a fight to those who were encroaching upon it. The U.S. government and those who engulfed the continent for the most part turned a blind eye to the plight of the Native American cultures.

A final myth is that the Oregon Trail was simply a corridor conveying a people from one coast to another. At first, most people thought that the interior of the continent, generally referred to as the "Great American Desert," was uninhabitable. But during the 1840s, this notion was gradually dispelled. In 1842, Congress appointed the young, ambitious surveyor and geographer Lieutenant John Charles Frémont to explore the West. Frémont's journey from Westport, Missouri, through South Pass in the Rocky Mountains to the Columbia River in Oregon opened the eyes of the nation to new possibilities. Frémont's narrative and map, published a year later in 1843, provided just what was needed for westward expansion: an accurate guide. It was Frémont's wife, Jesse Benton (daughter of Senator Thomas Hart Benton), who polished his reports, thus providing a readable guide for even the inexperienced westbound travelers along what became the Great Platte River Road, or Oregon Trail.

That same year saw another momentous event. In 1843 wagons finally made it over the mountains into Oregon and California. In previous years, emigrants had traveled west, but they were forced to abandon their wagons east of the mountains. So the development of wagon routes *through* the mountains signaled the official start of westward expansion.

In 1843 and again in 1845, Lieutenant Frémont set off on additional westward expeditions. In the succeeding years, he published two more reports of his travels. The nation was captivated by Frémont's accounts of the West, and by the late 1840s the American frontier was well on its way to disappearing.

But it was not the early explorers or the emigrants who had truly first defined the Oregon Trail. The Trail began with migratory animals following the path of least resistance to water sources. Then came the Indians, hunting game. Next came explorers, trappers, and traders. Following on their heels were the missionaries taking the westward paths in search of souls to save. As soon as it was proven that wagons could make it over the cross-continental path, emigrants chose to follow their own dreams of a better life, for the West had become a symbol of health, wealth, and freedom. Today, almost all traces of the Oregon Trail are covered by railroads and highways, as is evidenced by Interstate 80, which crosses the nation.

What was it that separated those who chose to travel 2,170 miles to the Pacific Ocean over the Oregon Trail from those who never entertained such a notion? No one knows. Only the stories of some of those who chose to make the journey remain to speak of that decision and its impact in settling the West. It was an exhausting trek that these hardy and headstrong souls took as they pushed wearily onward. The path led some to a land that realized their dreams and aspirations. For others, it took them to their graves.

The faith and determination of these brave men, women, and children to overcome any obstacle, physical or emotional, enabled most of them to succeed in reaching their destinations. The tenacity, fortitude, courage, and adventuresome spirit of the emigrants and immigrants in the largest mass migration in this country's history remain unrivaled. Their reasons for taking on the Trail may have been simple, but it is the complexity of the journey that intrigues us today.

This book offers an insight into the life stories of twenty-nine heroic individuals, who, with or without the support of their families, ventured into lands unknown. All the stories are true and are substantiated with facts and details uncovered by extensive research, including the author's conversations and interviews with the emigrants' descendants. On occasion, when specific facts were not available, details were added that reflect conditions of the times.

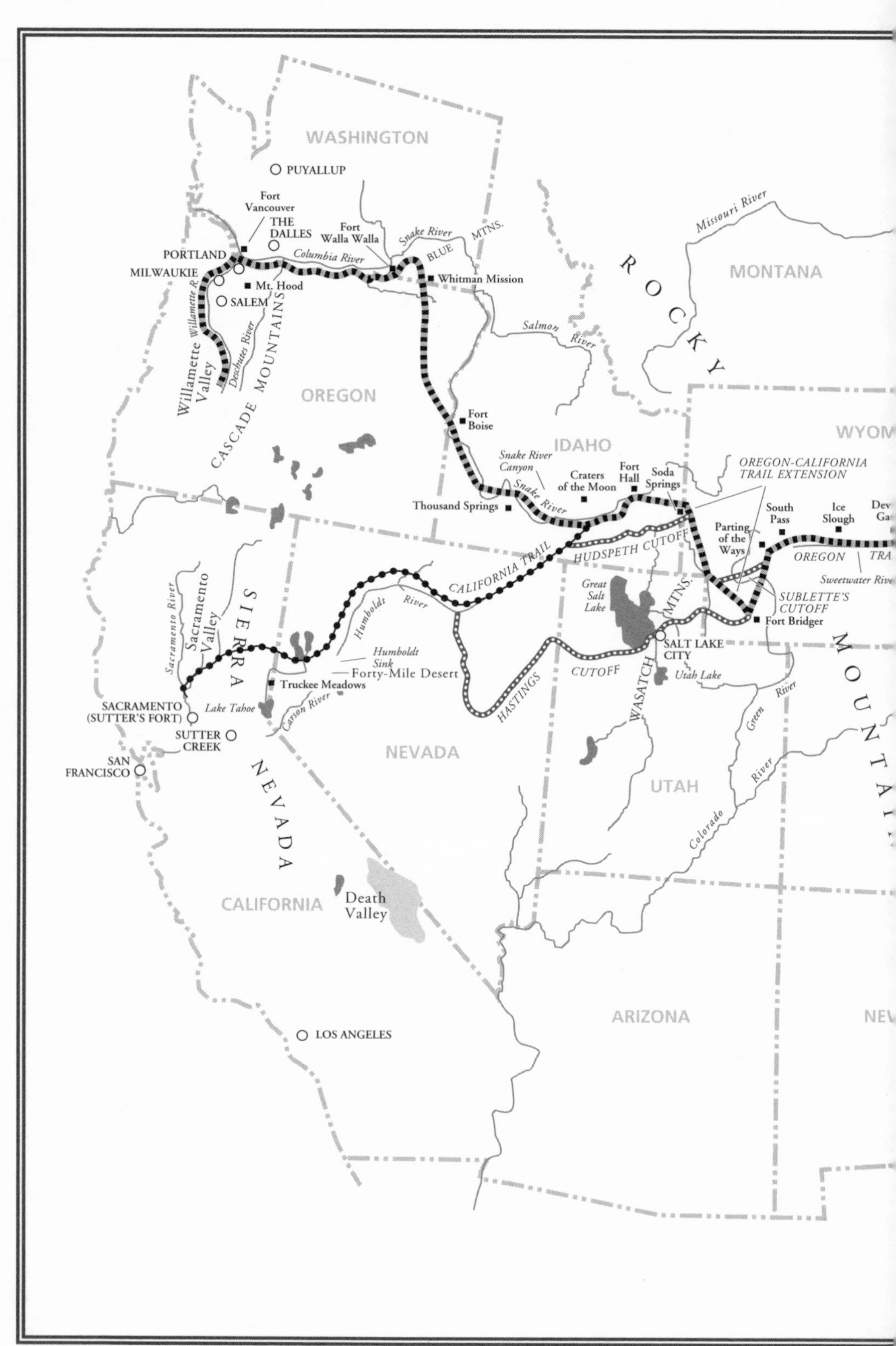

WASHINGTON
PUYALLUP
Fort Vancouver
THE DALLES
Fort Walla Walla
PORTLAND
MILWAUKIE
Columbia River
Snake River
BLUE MTNS.
Whitman Mission
Mt. Hood
SALEM
Willamette R.
Deschutes River
Willamette Valley
CASCADE MOUNTAINS
OREGON
Salmon River
Missouri River
MONTANA
ROCKY
MOUNTAINS
Fort Boise
IDAHO
WYOM
Snake River Canyon
Snake River
Craters of the Moon
Fort Hall
Soda Springs
OREGON-CALIFORNIA TRAIL EXTENSION
Thousand Springs
South Pass
Ice Slough
Parting of the Ways
OREGON TRA
Sweetwater Rive
HUDSPETH CUTOFF
CALIFORNIA TRAIL
Great Salt Lake
MTNS.
SUBLETTE'S CUTOFF
Fort Bridger
SALT LAKE CITY
Sacramento River
Sacramento Valley
SIERRA NEVADA
Humboldt River
Humboldt Sink
Forty-Mile Desert
Truckee Meadows
HASTINGS CUTOFF
WASATCH
Utah Lake
Green River
SACRAMENTO (SUTTER'S FORT)
Lake Tahoe
Carson River
SUTTER CREEK
SAN FRANCISCO
NEVADA
UTAH
Colorado River
CALIFORNIA
Death Valley
ARIZONA
LOS ANGELES

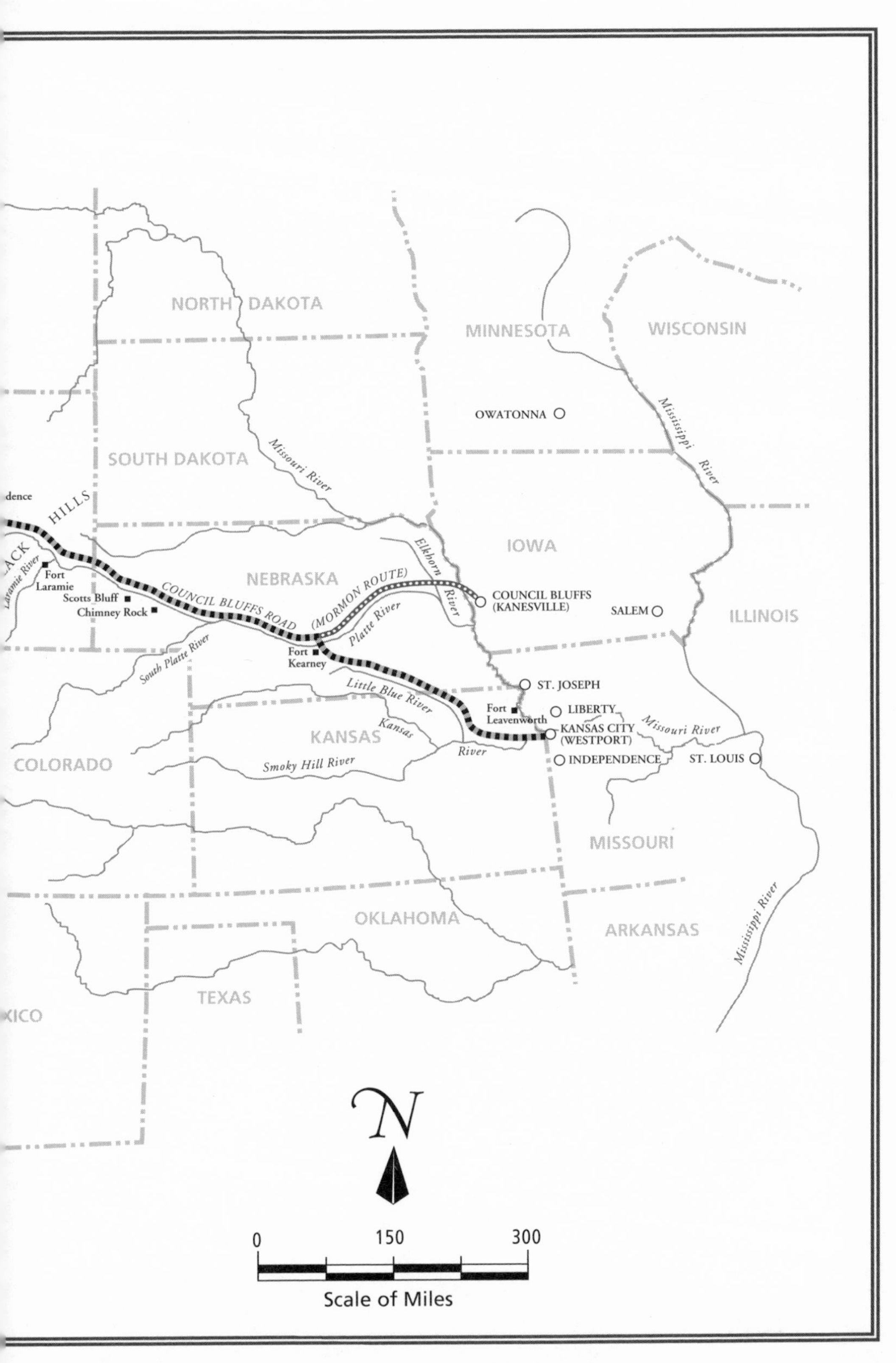

NORTH DAKOTA
MINNESOTA
WISCONSIN
OWATONNA
SOUTH DAKOTA
Missouri River
Mississippi River
dence
BLACK HILLS
IOWA
NEBRASKA
Elkhorn River
Laramie River
Fort Laramie
Scotts Bluff
Chimney Rock
COUNCIL BLUFFS ROAD
(MORMON ROUTE)
COUNCIL BLUFFS (KANESVILLE)
SALEM
ILLINOIS
Platte River
South Platte River
Fort Kearney
ST. JOSEPH
Little Blue River
Fort Leavenworth
LIBERTY
KANSAS CITY (WESTPORT)
Missouri River
Kansas River
KANSAS
COLORADO
Smoky Hill River
INDEPENDENCE
ST. LOUIS
MISSOURI
OKLAHOMA
ARKANSAS
Mississippi River
TEXAS
XICO
N
0
150
300
Scale of Miles

Almost within Reach

• Early 1800s •

On bended knee the young brave locked eyes with the mysterious, fearless Indian staring back at him from the pool of water. He noticed an irregular scar over the Indian's left eye, which denoted the warrior's bravery, and the firm jaw that represented undaunted determination. Holding his own stare, the unflinching brave lifted his arm high above his head, clenching his tomahawk as if to demonstrate his well-defined arm muscles. The unsmiling Indian did the same, and then both lowered their tomahawks simultaneously to the earth without so much as blinking.

When the young brave crouched down and cupped his hands to drink from the basin of the collected spring waters, the image before him disappeared as his reflection was obliterated by the rippling effect of the water. Savoring the cool, refreshing drink, the brave stood and turned to face his tribe. He was ready.

The elders of the tribe, along with all the braves, were assembled to witness the handsome Sioux brave who had answered the invitation of the much-revered Sioux chieftain. Though many of the young Indians claimed to be able to perform the near-impossible feat set before them, the bragging rights would belong only to the one who could prove his strength and skill—by climbing the formidable rock formation.

When it came time to lay down his spear in front of the chief to symbolically declare that he had accepted the challenge, the lone brave showed no sign of emotion, doubt, or timidity. The warrior's courage and the confidence he exuded must have impressed the chief. Time would tell if this young Sioux was fit to be the leader of his people one day. The brave's challenge loomed over all the spectators—none other than the massive natural formation that in later years would be called Chimney Rock.

Rising up out of the landscape and standing erect along the Platte River, Chimney Rock was foreboding. The impressive monument was composed mostly of hardened Brule clay intermixed with volcanic ash along with layers of red and white sandstone. It reached some 500 feet into the sky. Not one person was known to have successfully scaled its height, but those who had attempted to climb some portion of the well-known landmark had been rewarded with a sweeping panoramic view of the environs below.

The young brave followed six steps behind the Sioux leader in a rhythmic dance around the half-mile circumference of the base of the great Chimney Rock. Then, to the chanting of his tribesmen and the beating of drums, the brave bowed before the inverted funnel-shaped dome of massive rock. Raising his head, his eyes traveled upward past the cone-shaped center, which gave way to a vertical spire extending into the heavens.

The brave who could reach the pinnacle and stand as one with the sky would be given the gift of a much-coveted colt. The Sioux were known as exceptional horsemen, and such a reward from the chief would bring honor to the victor's family as well as great personal esteem. A horse was needed not only to hunt the great buffalo, but also to better enable a warrior to "count coup," or touch a living enemy in battle, a most courageous act. Honor in battle brought the attainment of manhood, which, along with the accumulation of horses, was needed before a brave could take a wife.

Dressed only in footwear and a loincloth, the young brave looked down at his buckskin moccasins with their beaded symbol of the sun. He shifted his weight from one foot to the other, stirring up a cloud of dust, and felt the weight of the task set before him.

The worn leather soles of his moccasins conformed perfectly to the contours of his feet, which had always enabled him to find a secure grip. The brave closed his eyes and envisioned himself scaling the nearby bluffs, for that practice had made him a swift and agile climber. Next he shook his long, brawny arms to relax his muscles. He kicked some loose chunks from around the base of the rock, grunted, and began the long ascent.

The broad base of Chimney Rock actually made for easy climbing, and his agility made the climb look effortless. As the brave approached the midsection of the rock, he could feel the heat of the midday sun intensely, and his well-defined body glistened with perspiration. He contorted himself into far-reaching positions yet gracefully clambered upward, fingering the sides of the rock for small crevices to grasp. The malleable clay could be easily sculpted, and when the brave could not manipulate it manually, he reached for his tomahawk in a rawhide sling around his waist and cut notches into the rock.

At times the crumbling pieces fell, making him feel rather precariously perched as his body, caked in a pasty dust, clung to the rocks. From far below it looked as if his leg had slipped, but he had only extended it to work out a cramp.

The brave was so intent on reaching the summit that he had not realized how high he had climbed. The steady beating of his heart nearly drowned out the drums that had been urging him on.

On the vertical ascent of the third and final section of the monolith, he had to carefully chisel each handhold in the narrowing spire. The beads of perspiration dropping from the

Indian onto the cocoa-colored clay created reddish-brown freckles on the rock's surface. Onward he pressed. Several grueling hours later the pinnacle of Chimney Rock was in sight.

The brave's heart was filled with pride and his head with visions of being bestowed a great honor. He may have imagined himself becoming a legend in his own tribe and even in those of his enemies, the Crow and the Pawnee. He carefully etched the last few notches in the rock with his tomahawk. Then, just as he was about to pull himself to the very top, pieces of the soft clay that had been crumbling down gave way. His footed moccasin slipped off the fractured notch and the brave plummeted to his death, to the shock and horror of all those assembled.

According to custom, a platform grave was erected on four posts reaching 8 feet high. The remains of the proud young brave were wrapped in a blanket and laid atop the scaffolding. Interring the dead in this manner allowed the deceased to be closer to the Great Spirit and also offered protection from scavenging animals. After the body decayed, the bones would be brought back for a ceremonial burial and placed in a tribal tomb. To honor the fallen Indian, the chief had his tribesmen erect the wooden scaffold near the Chimney Rock that claimed the brave's life. Legend has it that the chief ordered the coveted colt, which rightfully belonged to the brave who had come so close to the pinnacle, to be killed in order to accompany the young warrior into the spirit world.

The legends and lore that surround Chimney Rock were part of the plains people's history long before the great wave of emigration engulfed the land. Seen for miles in the distance, Chimney Rock not only marked the end of the plains and the beginning of the more rugged mountainous terrain; it also intrigued all who passed by. Fur traders had come to refer to the oddly shaped natural rock formation as "the Chimney," and emigrants who followed along the Oregon Trail in the 1840s dubbed it "Chimney Rock." Some 600 miles down the Trail,

Chimney Rock was the most recognized and first of the eagerly anticipated landmarks, if not the very symbol of the Oregon Trail.

Though no one else is known to have scaled its summit, thousands of emigrants left their mark by carving their names in the soft Brule clay of Chimney Rock. This evidence did not remain for long, however; the erosive forces of nature continually wore away all such traces.

What can be seen today around the base of Chimney Rock are pieces of the great crumbling landmark. These chunks continue to tumble down, keeping the legend of the nameless Sioux Indian brave alive.

A Man All Alone

•1828•

It was an eerie evening for the weary band of travelers encamped near Scotts Bluff, a mammoth landmark along the Oregon Trail. The wide-eyed emigrants, both young and old, huddled together around the dancing flames of their evening campfire. They sat motionless underneath the blanket of the cool night air with the stars twinkling above them as they listened intently. The tragedy that had befallen one Hiram Scott at this well-known bluff in present-day western Nebraska had caused his comrades to name this natural geologic wonder after him, and the story of Scott's fate captivated the fancy of all the travelers on the Oregon Trail. The sudden, shrill howling of coyotes in the distance sent a chill up and down the spines of the group at the campsite, yet no one moved for fear of missing a word of the unbelievable story.

Scotts Bluff was a colossal fortress of natural sandstone and clay towering some 800 feet above the south bank of the Platte River. This natural formation marked the end of the Great Plains for the emigrants; mountainous terrain lay ahead, and the bluff posed one of the first challenges in the new landscape. The caravans could either go 5 miles around the bluff or pass through a narrow gash in its center, taking a circuitous path through the soft stone where the wagon ruts were worn 8 feet deep by continuous use. No matter how they chose to bypass the great bluff, nearly all camped near it and heard the story of its naming.

Twenty-three-year-old Hiram Scott was a mountain man, and mountain men were by nature independent souls who withdrew to the mountains to ply their trade in the great outdoors. These rugged trappers, hunters, and fur traders preferred a life of relative solitude, making their living off the land. An ad placed in the *Missouri Gazette* caught the attention of the young and carefree Scott, who signed on as a fur trapper for the Rocky Mountain Fur Company. He found that the work suited him just fine, and he became one of the company's more dependable men. Hiram Scott and James B. Bruffee worked as clerks or field commanders for a supply caravan. They, along with other brigades of fur trappers, made their way across the mountainous terrain hunting and trapping animals for their pelts.

The mountain men crossed the Platte River Valley to meet at the annual summer rendezvous, which attracted a multitude of trappers—white men and Indians alike. At the rendezvous they traded animal pelts for money, food, whiskey, beads, and other luxuries. The trappers then made their way east to St. Louis, Missouri, with the best of their pelts for sale. Bypassing the massive bluffs located along the river became standard procedure.

In 1828 Scott, his partner, Bruffee, and the other fur trappers came out of the mountains with their pelts after enduring a blizzard and a skirmish with the Indians. On their way to the Green River rendezvous, Scott became ill, perhaps as a result of those encounters. As the trappers headed east after the rendezvous, Scott's condition worsened and he became incapacitated.

When Scott was unable to ride his horse any farther, the travelers decided to transport him by water. His company split up and two companions planned to take the infirm Scott down the Platte River in a makeshift "bull-boat." This was a vessel constructed from animal hides stretched over a wooden framework. While they traveled downriver, Scott's partner James B. Bruffee would lead the rest of the party overland. The plan was to meet at the massive bluff on the south bank of the North Platte River.

Capable of carrying several hundred pounds, the waterproof bull-boat was buoyant but could not be steered easily. The mountain men entered the river and attempted to maneuver their way through the waters, only to have their boat capsize as they went through rapids. Remarkably, the able-bodied trappers managed to save their invalid friend and themselves from going under, and they all made it safely to shore. In the disaster, however, their guns, ammunition, and meager supplies were lost. Trying again to transport Scott on land became a desperate and almost insurmountable task, made worse because they now had no way to procure any food. Exhausted, famished, and far behind schedule, the men forced themselves to push forward on foot, inching their way along in a seemingly futile attempt to reunite with the rest of their party.

To their bitter disappointment and utter disbelief, after they had mustered the strength to reach the agreed-upon location, there was no one there. Bruffee, the likely leader of the caravan, had not kept his word to wait for them. Why the main company did not wait at the agreed-upon meeting spot remains a mystery to this day. Perhaps the advance company needed to move on to find food. Perhaps their nine-day delay had caused the main company to think that Scott and his two caretakers had died. Thinking that Scott and his two companions were coming down the river, maybe it never occurred to the lead trappers to backtrack overland to check for any sight of them. Or, if greed entered into the equation, arriving late in St. Louis might have robbed the trappers of their chance to get the most for their pelts.

Scott's comrades were overburdened as they carried their sick and injured friend. With little energy left due to fatigue and the lack of food, they had an agonizing decision to make. They could stay with Scott and all three perish together, or they could abandon him to his fate to save themselves. Without their charge, the two companions could perhaps catch up with the main outfit and restore their own health. Scott's suffering indicated that he would not recover without proper care and food and, consequently, his companions abandoned him to die.

The following summer the young trapper's remains and personal effects were identified after being found miles from where the travelers had left him. William Sublette, of Smith, Jackson, & Sublette (the fur company for which Scott had worked), gathered Scott's bones and buried him there at the bluff. Little did Scott know that the unfortunate circumstance of his own death would be marked for all time by having the majestic bluff along the North Platte River named in his honor.

There are more than sixty accounts of Scott's tragic story mentioned in journals or diaries of emigrants who passed by what came to be known as Scotts Bluff on the Oregon Trail. The earliest accounts of the incident, such as the one retold here, were written just a few years afterward and perhaps come closest to the truth. After years of retelling, the facts may have become embellished or distorted. For instance, some versions of Scott's fate claim that he died of disease or hunger, or that he was a solitary trapper who lost his way and died a lonely death. According to Hiram Daniel Scott, a descendant of the renowned trapper, the Scott family believes that the elder Hiram was killed by a grizzly bear. This could explain why his remains were found so far from where he was deserted. However, most accounts generally attest to a young trapper being abandoned by his companions, with his remains being recovered later. Though a diary entry written in 1834 claims to know the identity of one "soulless villain" who abandoned Scott, the name was never revealed.

After the initial shock of hearing about the young trapper in the prime of his life being abandoned and left to die, the emigrants may have taken a closer look at each other as they sat huddled around their evening campfire. It must have been inconceivable to think of leaving a fellow traveling companion behind. If, as some believed, Scott's spirit resided at the bluff, it is unlikely that anyone drifted off to sleep without thinking of the ghostly legend that surrounded Scott's mournful fate.

Over the River or Through the Woods

• 1843 •

The Applegate family was about to find out firsthand that the final leg of the Oregon Trail was the most dangerous. Upon reaching The Dalles, an important trading center and a place of rocky rapids along the Columbia River, the emigrants had to make a decision. They could painstakingly lead their wagons around the river through the dense woods on Mt. Hood, or take a chance rafting down the tumultuous Columbia River to reach their destination in the Willamette Valley. At this point, near the end of their 2,000-mile journey, the bone-weary emigrants could hardly muster the energy to choose.

It was in early November when the Applegates, having chosen the water route, gathered at the banks of the Columbia River. It had taken several weeks for the men in the party to construct enough wooden flatboats for all 120 wagons.

The time had come to divide into smaller groups and board their makeshift rafts. Everyone must have secretly wondered just who would win this battle—man or nature?—for they sensed this was a river like no other. The emigrants lowered their skiffs and pushed off into the Columbia River, hoping for the best.

Seven-year-old Jesse Applegate's raft took the lead. There were eight people on his raft, including an Indian who was hired on as a guide in Fort Walla Walla to pilot them downriver. On board were Jesse's parents, Lindsay and Elizabeth Applegate, his baby brother, and his Aunt Cynthia and Uncle Jesse and their baby.

The second raft, which followed directly behind Jesse's, held six people. William Parker and William Doke, both in their early twenties, manned the oars. Jesse's two brothers, Elisha, age eleven, and Warren, age nine, along with their cousin Edward, also nine years old, held on for dear life. Seventy-year-old Alexander McClellen (endearingly called Uncle Mac) made sure the young boys stayed put.

At first young Jesse was enthralled by the whirlpools and the white crests of foaming waves that rocked his raft on this breathtaking ride. It even seemed a luxury to be carried swiftly along as others were laboriously traversing a narrow footpath through the uncleared Cascade Mountain Range alongside the river. No one knew that the Columbia River, though full of life, had yet to show its true colors.

The mothers with their babes in their arms swayed with the gyrating motion of the raft, which seemed to rise up and down and back and forth simultaneously. Miraculously, the riders stayed aboard. Taking his cues from the forced placid faces of the adults on board and the peaceful countenances of the slumbering little ones, Jesse breathed deeply to calm himself, though his eyes were as wide as saucers.

At times Jesse could make out his cousin and brothers on the raft behind him, only to lose sight of them under the crests of the waves. It was when the roar of the raging water took on a thunderous tone that Jesse's heart leapt.

By degrees the river deviated from its westward course, taking a northwesterly direction as the skiffs floated along. The bend was angled just enough to act as an explosive bottleneck ready to spew forth both water and rafts. The Indian pilot was expertly guiding Jesse's raft to avoid any such perils, and all the rafts were to follow the course he took.

Jesse noticed that the breakers ahead blocked out any

further view of the rapids downriver. The Indian guide hunkered down to find his center of gravity amid the thunderbolt of breaking waves crashing down upon them. The emigrants took this as a prudent thing to do and followed in like fashion to steady themselves.

Holding on for dear life, Jesse's small hands grasped the splintered sides of his raft. He looked around the other rafts to see how everyone was doing. The turbulent water gushed aboard Jesse's raft and disengaged everyone on it from their positions. The passengers scrambled to grab hold of anything or anybody to avoid being swept overboard into the raging river. Jesse was drenched to the skin. His eyes were ablaze with fear and his body trembled from both the numbing cold of the water and the terror of it all.

The ride was frighteningly exhilarating for Jesse, yet a sense of dread set in. His tattered raft was roughly 20 yards from the north shore when Jesse noticed that the smaller raft behind them had been swept off course. It had gotten caught in the strong current and ended up across the river near the south bank, far from the safe channel that the pilot was heading for.

For the briefest moment the waters seemed to calm themselves. Then in wielding its power and showing off its whitecaps and ruthless currents, the Columbia River came alive again. It took on the form of a sea monster that rose up whole from the earth, only to crash back down again. The force was enough to throw all that was on its watery back upward. When the ramshackle rafts came crashing down, their contents, emigrants included, were violently flung about. Amazingly, the Indian pilot, Jesse, his parents, and his Uncle Jesse and Aunt Cynthia and the babies were surviving each tumultuous upheaval.

The Columbia River was foaming at the mouth, reducing everyone's vision by a barely penetrable wall of white spray. Jesse made out the bodies of his brothers, Elisha and Warren, and his cousin, Edward, on the other raft as they were pitched upward only to fall back down. Their death grips were the only things keeping them aboard.

Suddenly, the piercing cries of Jesse's mother and aunt could be heard above the screams and shouts emanating from those on the toss-turned rafts. The sheer panic in their voices relayed the horror that they were witnessing and the terror of it all paralyzed young Jesse.

They could only watch in abject fear as the current whirled the nearly vertical raft behind them as if it were caught in a cyclone. With a horrendous roaring noise, the raft was sucked under the water by the powerful whirlpool for the first time. The once exciting, now terrifying, river had literally swallowed up the raft that Jesse had just seen moments ago. After hitting the bottom of the riverbed, the raft was catapulted upward—amazingly with all of its crew except young Warren.

Jesse's father and uncle saw their sons' raft go under. Without a moment's hesitation they dropped their oars and lunged toward the edge of their own unsteady raft, preparing to dive in. Jesse's mother and aunt desperately clung to their husbands. With every ounce of conviction, they implored the men to realize the insanity of going into the river. They begged them not to make a rash decision that in all likelihood would not only be futile, but would leave them widowed and unprotected in an unsettled land.

While everything surely happened at lightning speed as the horrifying scene unfolded, it seemed to Jesse as if this new, chaotic turn of events was occurring in slow motion. He watched in disbelief as the mad river swallowed up his brothers' raft for a second time—this time tossing everyone still on it into the water. Jesse's own skiff careened out of sight as the wild water carried it farther downstream. He could see nothing more and feared that everyone on the second raft had been sucked under by the whirlpool. Meanwhile Jesse's own raft nearly crashed into a large protruding rock, which would have thrown them all overboard, had not Jesse's father and uncle taken up their oars to assist the Indian pilot at that exact moment.

When Jesse's raft landed downriver at a break in the ragged shoreline, the distraught family and friends clambered out of their skiff and up the riverbank. They ran along the shoreline, desperately searching for any sign of their lost loved ones, not knowing who had survived the ordeal. Acting impulsively, Jesse's father grabbed his gun and aimed it at the Indian pilot, whom he perceived to be reckless. In a state of frenzied grief, he needed to put the blame on someone. The Indian perceptively made his escape to the safety of the woods, never to return.

The band searched desperately on shore until they heard news of survivors from someone who had run ahead. Jesse's brother Elisha had jumped from the top of the vertical raft before it went down for a second time. He and William Parker were able to stay afloat by grasping a featherbed ticking that was part of the flotsam and jetsam sweeping by. Though weak from exertion, they were swept to an island and managed to crawl across a scanty causeway to the safety of the shore. William Doke managed to survive by grasping a passing raft just moments before reaching the second set of rapids.

The insidious Columbia River did not rest until it had claimed the lives of the others. Jesse's brother Warren was never seen after the first time his raft went down. Alexander McClellen, the family friend nicknamed "Uncle Mac," rescued Jesse's cousin, Edward, by placing him on some oars that chanced to be floating by, only to miss the point of land. Both went under. The bodies of Warren, Uncle Mac, and Edward never surfaced again after losing out to the second whirlpool. Though the families searched in vain, the deceased were never found.

Jesse and his remaining family members and friends eventually made it safely to the Willamette Valley. However, as part of the Great Migration of 1843, which brought more than 1,000 emigrants west that year, the Applegate family's traumatic entry into the new land was not unique. Until a defined route was established, forging a path through the woods took its toll on many weary emigrants, and traveling by river proved to be a dance with death. Losing loved ones at the Trail's end—so close to their destination—nearly depleted the settlers of their energy and enthusiasm for their new homeland. But the challenges and risks inherent in the cross-country trek were still not enough to deter the multitudes of determined emigrants who were to make their way over the Oregon Trail.

Having each lost a son to the perils of the Columbia River, Jesse Applegate's father and uncle vowed to find a safer route to the Willamette Valley. Three years later, in 1846, they forged a new path through Nevada, northern Cailfornia, and southern Oregon, which came to be known as the Applegate Trail.

For Better or for Worse

•1845•

Truly, what could be more exciting for a brood of children than to learn that they were to embark on a cross-country trek that required them to camp outdoors for months on end? The year was 1845 and forty-four-year-old Daniel and forty-two-year-old Elizabeth (Betsey) Bayley fit the profile of the typical emigrants traveling the Oregon Trail. Most emigrants were from the Midwest and most were farmers. Before transplanting to Oregon, the Bayleys moved from Ohio to Savannah, Missouri, but Mr. Bayley had entertained the notion of farming "much farther west" one day. Most emigrant families also had children under the age of fifteen. The Bayley children were spaced like rungs on a ladder: Timothy, age fifteen; Caroline, age thirteen; Miranda, age eleven; Bishop Asbury, age six; Zernia, age four; Iola, age two; and Delphine, an infant.

In 1845 the entire Bayley family departed from their home in Missouri and headed toward their new home in Chehalem Valley, Oregon. Though the average cross-country trek took between four and five months in a covered wagon, it would take the Bayley family seven months and twenty-one days to travel the Oregon Trail to their final destination. The Bayleys' overland journey was marked by events that ran the gamut from exhilarating to life-threatening to preposterous.

Of all the adventures that the Oregon Trail could offer, perhaps the most intriguing for the children was the opportunity to be near the much-talked-of Indians. The Bayley clan eagerly anticipated any exchange with the Indians, but little did thirteen-year-old Caroline realize that she would be the focal point in such an exchange some 1,000 miles into their journey.

Shortly after pulling into Fort Hall, along the Snake River in present-day southeastern Idaho, the Bayleys had their first encounter with Indians. The fort's dilapidated adobe buildings served as a place where emigrants could secure provisions and seek advice about the trail ahead. The many Indians gathered there were interested in new and unfamiliar objects and were eager to trade fish, moccasins, and buckskins for almost any emigrant trinket.

While most of the Indians were interested in obtaining emigrant clothing, especially men's shirts, the Indians at Fort Hall when the Bayleys were there had their sights set on quite another commodity—wives. For the prized possession of an emigrant wife, they were willing to trade horses—a trade that to the Indians seemed entirely fair. It seemed outrageous to the emigrants, particularly the female contingent, but Daniel Bayley found it rather humorous. That is where the problem began. Perhaps it was just Daniel Bayley's sense of humor, or simply an ill-thought-out attempt to relate to the Indians gathered at the fort. Whatever the case, it prompted him to make an offer that was to go down in Bayley history.

A handsome young brave had taken quite an interest in the young and pretty Caroline Bayley. Daniel Bayley picked up on this and apparently thought he would have some fun with the information. The proud and jovial father jokingly asked the young Indian how many horses he would be willing to trade for his eldest daughter, saying, "Give me six horses and you can have her." Whether or not the blushing Caroline found the proposed offer as humorous as did her father has been lost over time. All joking aside, the interaction between the Bayleys and the Indians was at the very least memorable.

Who knows what went through young Caroline's mind that night as she lay in the relative security of her family's camp at Fort Hall? Resting under the evening stars, surrounded by strangers, strange customs, and strange offers, Caroline was most likely very eager to continue the journey the next day. The following morning was busy and hectic, as everyone prepared to break camp. Perhaps the Bayleys were too busy finishing up their typical trail breakfast of coffee, bacon, and hardtack (dry biscuits) to notice the approaching Indian.

At first hardly anyone paid attention to the Indian riding through the fort—that is, until they noticed what was behind him. Riding through the assembled crowd of people at the fort was the handsome brave from the day before, wearing a serious expression. Trailing behind him were six of the finest horses anyone had ever seen. To the astonishment of Caroline and her father, the Indian had sought them out and was making his way toward them. Clearly, he was intent on seeing through the trade he had proposed a day ago.

It was too late to make a run for it. This was one determined-looking Indian. There was not one ounce of joking left in the suddenly solemn Mr. Bayley. He must have had to do some explaining to Mrs. Bayley, who had quickly caught on to the young Indian's intention.

The reluctant prospective bride most likely retreated to the relative safe haven of the family's covered wagon, leaving her father to deal with the unbelievable turn of events. Even with the brave willing to prove how worthy his horses were, and how fair the trade was, the Bayleys were not interested. The essence of Mr. Bayley's conversation was "No swap, no swap," which the Indian understood but was not about to accept.

Daniel Bayley tried in vain to explain that his offer had been made in jest, but the Indian would not take "no" for an answer. A standstill ensued. Not knowing what else to do, the nervous father-of-the-bride-to-be urged his oxen to start up—

after making sure all his children were accounted for. The Bayleys fell into formation behind their sixty-four-wagon caravan, which was pulling out. It's not hard to imagine all the children peeking out from the tightened circle of canvas at the rear hoop of their wagon to see what would happen next.

The children must have watched in disbelief as the lone Indian, trailing his six fine horses behind him, followed the Bayleys for miles and miles. When the Bayleys stopped to eat, the Indian stopped to eat. When they camped for the night, he camped for the night. When they started along the trail in the morning, he started along the trail. This dance went on for several days, during which Mr. Bayley endured a verbal beating from his wife.

When at long last the Indian lengthened his distance and dejectedly fell off the trail, only then could the Bayleys breathe a sigh of relief, especially Caroline. This was more excitement than anyone had bargained for. As Caroline's mother, Betsey, wrote in a letter to her sister four years later, "The Indians never joke, and Mr. Bayley took good care ever after not to joke with them."

The story of Caroline's marriage proposal was passed from generation to generation in the Bayley family. It also made its way into Oregon folklore, and along with it grew the account of the event. Legend had it that not six horses but sixty were offered as a trade. One version even had Caroline being rescued from an Indian camp by the men in her wagon train. As late as 1911 the *Portland Oregonian* was still printing stories of the pioneer Bayleys and their escapades along the Oregon Trail. Caroline Bayley did go on to marry in her new homeland in Oregon—twice in fact—but neither husband was an Indian.

The Way Home

•1845•

Forty-year-old Stephen H. L. Meek had years of experience trapping the rivers in the Oregon Territory as a mountain man. Perhaps he had felt that was enough to qualify him to offer his services as a paid guide to the emigrants who were bent on traveling west on whatever semi-established trails were available.

Meek felt quite pleased in 1845 when he secured the post of pilot, an elected position, to guide a very sizable emigrant caravan to the land called Oregon. Men like Meek who wanted to be guides went to the jumping-off towns along the Missouri River and tried to convince the emigrants that they would be the best guide. Meek arrived on the scene with letters of recommendation from notable mountain men, he offered some degree of experience, and he charged $250 for his services. As a result, he was elected by the emigrants over a Mr. Adams, who wanted to charge $300 but offered considerably less experience.

Meek was even more overjoyed when he became engaged to Elizabeth Schoonover, a young Canadian girl who was heading west, and after a week's acquaintance they were married. Soon afterward, however, Meek's troubles began. Some say Meek was incompetent; some say he was unlucky. The truth most likely lies somewhere in between. On the Trail, the fine line between success and failure was often determined by how much luck one had, but when luck didn't go your way, the results could be disastrous.

The ever-hopeful mountain-man-turned-emigrant-guide learned firsthand that it was difficult to keep a large group together as a cohesive unit. After one week, the caravan divided into three smaller companies, as often happened along the Trail when several men wanted leadership roles. Somehow Meek managed to retain the position of head pilot for this rather fluid train for better than half of the trip to Oregon. Meek's services were then terminated, perhaps because there were too many leaders and not enough followers in this particular group of emigrants. Needing to find employment, Meek rode ahead with his young wife to Fort Boise, a trading post where emigrants gathered. At Fort Boise (in present-day western Idaho), he conceived what he thought was a brilliant, albeit unproven, plan—a shortcut to the Willamette Valley in Oregon.

Meek's idea was to open a route heading west across the Oregon desert, find a passage through the Cascade Mountains large enough for wagons, and then follow the Willamette River north to The Dalles, an important trading center on the Columbia River. Meek asserted that the proposed route would save 150 to 200 miles, and that it could be accomplished in just thirty days. This bold assertion convinced emigrants gathered at Fort Boise to follow him. While some thought Meek's plan was preposterous, especially the idea of following a man whom they had just met and knew nothing about, others found the shortcut that bypassed the Blue Mountains along the Columbia River intriguing. Between 1,000 and 1,500 people—some 200 families in 480 wagons—signed up, and they set out on August 25 of 1845.

Soon after the hopeful emigrants set off from Fort Boise in a westerly direction, the terrain became progressively rougher. Shallow, rocky river bottoms made for difficult river crossings. The route had narrow valleys and high ridges that were hard on the oxen's hooves. Three to four footsore oxen, which were desperately needed, gave out each day. Between the rock-clearing, the poor grass for the animals, and the broken wagons, one emigrant commented that there was "more swaring then [sic] you ever heard." A collective sense of doubt and regret set in. Young Elizabeth Meek, wanting desperately to believe in her husband, could not avoid noticing the growing feelings of enmity toward him.

Piloting a large party over an unproven route was more difficult than Meek had anticipated. When water was hard to find, he suggested that the bulk of the caravan wait at camp while he led a party north to search for water. Instead, a group of one hundred disgruntled men insisted on heading west. Meek finally agreed to join them and led the search westward in vain for seven days, losing 80 miles in the quest for the life-saving liquid. Their throats were parched, and the blinding, choking dust stirred up by the wagons compounded the problem. The group finally conceded to go north as Meek had suggested, and they trudged onward. After a 25-mile stretch of waterless terrain, springs were eventually located, but not before the emigrants were absolutely irate.

Just past the two-thirds mark in their journey, animosity toward Meek began to increase daily, to the point that he had received several death threats. Everyone painfully realized that the shortcut was not at all short. The discontented travelers had lost their confidence in Meek and felt that he had no more knowledge of the country than they did. Rumors of ill will toward Meek caused him and his bride to hide in an emigrant's wagon for protection.

The frustrated companies became even more fragmented as the emigrants took matters into their own hands, with some heading off on whatever path Meek did not take. Strung out over 50 to 100 miles, the emigrants were unaware of one another's progress. Some who were not traveling with Meek thought that he had deserted them. Some who were traveling with him probably wished that he had. All were aiming to head north to rejoin the main Oregon Trail at The Dalles along the Columbia River.

By mid-September some emigrants were nearly out of provisions, so the weakened cattle were killed and eaten. Those companies who were out of food resorted to eating dead grasshoppers, salted grass, or whatever berries they could forage. The young ones, with their constant crying, could not understand why food was not forthcoming. Many companies began to travel at night so that the cattle could take advantage of the morning dew. "Mountain fever," a malady caused by fatigue and poor nutrition, began to claim the lives of the weakest victims, the young and the old. As one pioneer commented, ". . . so if misery loves company here is enough of it." Sapped of their strength, and plagued by the fear and worry of indecision, the emigrants were worn thin and had little resistance.

One lost, separated wagon train wandered about, desperately trying to find its way back to the main trail. These emigrants carved "the Lost Meeks, 1845" into a huge tree limb, hoping that by a miracle, someone would find them based on their forlorn signpost. Another misguided faction of the wandering Meek train discovered gold while digging in a dry creek bed for water. It was said that someone digging with a wooden blue bucket first noticed the gold, and the site eventually came to be known as "Blue Bucket Mine." But as the startled emigrants stared down at their amazing discovery, the truth rang painfully clear. The gold held no worth, for no amount of money could buy them what they most wanted—health, happiness, and a way home.

An enraged father who had lost his sons on the trip blamed Meek for their deaths and wanted revenge. Fearing for their lives, Meek and his young wife crossed over the treacherous Deschutes River and traveled with the aid of some local Indians for five days to The Dalles to secure help. There, they found that a relief party headed by the renowned Black Harris, a well-respected African-American mountaineer, had already started out to assist the lost party. It turned out that the emigrants from Fort Boise who had stayed on the main trail had arrived at The Dalles much earlier. They were worried about those who had taken Meek's cutoff. So Black Harris set out to find them.

The emigrants' condition was desperate. Two-thirds had run out of provisions and about fifty had perished. Black Harris and his men helped the emigrants convert their wagons to boats and constructed raft lines to cross the wild Deschutes. Mustering every ounce of energy that they had, the rescued emigrants arrived at The Dalles two weeks later. Many emigrants brought in were past the point of recovery and did not survive the ordeal. Some claim that up to seventy-five emigrants who chose to follow Meek lost their lives. The exhausted survivors were taken in at the nearby Methodist mission, which was totally unprepared for the onslaught of needy pioneers.

Those who had decided not to follow Meek and opted to stay on the main Oregon Trail arrived at The Dalles long ahead of Meek's party, with no apparent illness or unexpected difficulty. The Meek caravan was en route forty days longer than they would have been had they stayed on the main trail, and they went 400 to 500 miles out of their way. Regardless, no one's journey was over once they reached The Dalles. They all still faced 100 miles of travel either on or alongside the Columbia River to reach the Willamette Valley and the end of the Trail.

Perhaps Meek had been overly confident in taking a caravan where no wagons had ever been. Had 1845 not been such a dry year, had Meek been a stronger leader, had connections from one river to another been easily found, or had luck been on his side, then perhaps Stephen H. L. Meek would have faired better.

Years later the weatherworn tree limb bearing the words "the Lost Meeks, 1845" was discovered in a remote area and retrieved. It found a home in the Deschutes History Center in

Bend, Oregon, where it now resides. There it serves as a reminder of those who were desperately seeking their way home. Try as he did, Stephen Meek could not find it for them. The crude map that he had drawn proved to be no help at all. Meek led an expedition twenty-three years later in search of gold from the legendary Blue Bucket Mine. Once again luck was not with him, and the mine was never rediscovered.

Just One More Day
•1846•

Tamsen Donner was busy outfitting her daughters in their "uniforms for the plains," trading the girls' fancy clothes and dainty slippers for more practical outfits and footwear. Frances, Georgia Ann, and Eliza Donner (ages six, three, and two) were overjoyed to have clothes that they needn't worry about soiling as they traveled over the Oregon Trail. The Donners' preparation for their four-month trek across the continent with their friends the Reeds was all but complete.

Friends and loved ones wondered why these well-off families were leaving their privileged lives behind for a future of adventure and uncertainty. The forty-five-year-old mother, all of 5 feet tall and ninety-six pounds, thought that living primitively would be quite an adventure for everyone. She had written to her sister in Newburyport, Massachusetts, stating that she was "willing to go and have no doubt it will be an advantage to our children and to us." Tamsen Donner, an accomplished writer, had published some stories and poems and was eager to record an account of her trip in her journal. It was impossible for these high-spirited emigrants to have any idea of the travails that lay ahead.

George Donner, Tamsen's sixty-nine-year-old husband of ten years, along with his brother, had caught the "land fever," which drew people to the fertile farmland on the West Coast. Their friend James Reed had his own ambitions of working for the government handling "Indian relations" out west. The group decided to leave their homes in Springfield, Illinois, on April 15, 1846, and seek their fortunes in the West.

The Donner and Reed families, along with their employees (thirty-one people in all), had planned extensively for their journey. As the nine wagons of the three families proudly pulled out, people must have shaken their heads. The Donners' well-outfitted wagons paled in comparison to the Reeds' two-story "Pioneer Palace Car." This luxurious wagon sported cushioned seats on springs, a wood stove with its chimney through the canvas rooftop, a second-story bedroom, a large mirror, a library of books, and a side entrance. Few emigrants ever traveled in such grand style.

With Lansford Hastings's *The Emigrant's Guide to Oregon and California* as their bible, the party set out from Springfield, Illinois, to Independence, Missouri. There they would begin their long journey over the Oregon Trail into uncharted territory across rugged plains, blazing deserts, and steep mountains.

It was May 19 by the time they had traveled the 300 miles to Independence, where they joined up with another wagon train for protection. No one seemed the slightest bit concerned that they were a full month behind the recommended starting date for setting out over the Oregon Trail. (In reality, the overland journey was a race against time as emigrants needed to reach their final destination before inclement weather slowed or stopped them. On this beautiful spring day, it was hard to imagine such urgency.)

At first, crossing the Oregon Trail seemed rather uneventful, though, sadly, Grandmother Reed had died from chronic illness toward the end of May. Tamsen even wrote to her sister, saying, "I never could have believed we could have traveled so far with so little difficulty." As the company journeyed through the Nebraska Territory in June, more families joined their wagon train. Passing the landmarks mentioned in Hastings's guidebook, such as Chimney Rock and Scotts Bluff, reassured them that they were on the right path and all was well.

It was mid-July when their caravan reached a turning point that sealed the fate of the travelers over the Oregon–California Trail, dividing them both physically and emotionally. At Fort Laramie, a fur-trading post in present-day Wyoming, the suggestion of taking a time-saving cutoff brought dissension to the group.

Hastings Cutoff, recommended in the author's guidebook, sparked much heated debate among the men. Even though the original traces of the Oregon Trail came to be used less and less when various time-saving cutoffs were developed, Hastings Cutoff was risky because it had never been traveled by wagons. The trail left Fort Bridger (in present-day southwestern Wyoming) and went west from the Rocky Mountains, around the south side of the Great Salt Lake, and across the Forty-Mile Desert before crossing the Sierra Nevada into California. The thought of saving 350 to 400 miles was tempting enough to make travelers disregard the warnings of crossing the dry land.

At Fort Laramie the travelers consulted James Clyman, an experienced explorer returning from the West. Clyman warned the travelers to avoid taking the Hastings Cutoff at all costs. Clyman and another mountain man had joined Lansford Hastings earlier in the year to test the cutoff. Clyman had been outraged at its impassability for wagons—the land was waterless and the densely populated forest and steep ridges in the Wasatch Mountain Range were treacherous. In fact, he had felt so strongly about it that he had backtracked and warned advancing emigrants of the insanity of taking the shortcut. Clyman knew James Reed well from their years of service together in the Black Hawk War, and he hoped to convince Reed to heed his advice. He later wrote, "I told Reed to take the regular wagon track and never leave it—it's barely possible to get through if you follow it—and maybe impossible if you don't."

Despite the warnings, the decision was put to a vote. All the males over age fourteen gathered and voted. Some voted to take Hastings Cutoff; others heeded Clyman's warning and voted to stay on the main trail. The party decided to split into two groups. George Donner was elected captain of the group that was to take Hastings Cutoff, now calling themselves the Donner Party.

The Donners' teamster, Hiram Miller, strongly disagreed with James Reed's insistence on taking the unproven route to save time. Miller left the Donner Party to stay on the original trail. Tamsen Donner was described as "gloomy, sad, and dispirited in view of the fact that her husband and others could think for a moment of leaving the old road and confide in the statement of a man of whom they knew nothing, but was probably some selfish adventurer." Tamsen was infuriated at having no say in her own fate and that of her children.

After crossing the summit of the Rocky Mountains, both groups of emigrants descended into the Sandy River and reached the "Parting of the Ways." Here on July 31, the Donner Party left the main Oregon Trail and took the left fork to Fort Bridger and the Hastings Cutoff, which headed toward California.

Upon reaching Fort Bridger, which was the last place to secure provisions, the talk about Hastings Cutoff was positive. The proprietor of Fort Bridger, James Bridger, strongly promoted Hastings Cutoff, as he was interested in the business that the passing emigrants provided. Unfortunately, Bridger's partner neglected to give James Reed letters from his friend Edwin Bryant who had gone ahead on Hastings Cutoff and barely got through on a mule. In these letters, Bryant vehemently warned that there was no way a wagon could survive. All the Donner Party knew was that Lansford Hastings himself was guiding the first caravan of sixty wagons over the cutoff and had left just a few days earlier. Hastings had promised to backtrack and lead the Donner Party, but they decided to set out and catch up with him instead.

Within a week there was serious trouble. The touted Hastings Cutoff was hardly even a visible path through the wilderness. When the Donner Party arrived at the impassable Weber Canyon on August 6, they found a note from Hastings along with a crude map telling them to abandon the cutoff and stating that Hastings would return when he could to lead them on another route. It was too late to turn back, for they were already far behind schedule and the women were "mad with anger." The party was left with no choice but to hoist their caravan over the narrow precipices of Echo Canyon by taking apart and reassembling each wagon. Tamsen and the other women were well aware that they were only inches away from plunging off the cliffs as they lowered their children, supplies, and wagons with pulleys and ropes over the ledges. After reassembling their wagons, the pioneers agonizingly chopped tree after maddening tree at an incredibly retarded pace to clear a path.

In mid-August, their dispirited caravan was overtaken by a group of emigrants who had been following in their path for days and had finally caught up to them. Their twenty-three-wagon group now numbered eighty-seven people. Fortunately, four of the new members were able-bodied young men who joined them in hacking a way through the thickly forested canyon. Together they painstakingly averaged only 2 to 4 miles per day rather than the expected 15.

While crossing the Great Salt Lake Desert in early September, they ran out of water and begin to lose many of their oxen. Forced to abandon their wagons, some of the emigrants had to carry whatever supplies they could. They cached, or buried, some of their cargo for later retrieval. Food, supplies, and energy became dangerously low.

In mid-October they set out to cross the Forty-Mile Desert at the end of the Humboldt River. Along the way they were almost done in by thirst. Tamsen gave her children peppermint-soaked sugar lumps and flattened bullets to suck on to produce saliva. It was remarkable that she kept her young children alive and continually urged them on under such adverse conditions.

Once they made it through the desert, the weary party rested for a few days at Truckee Meadows (present day Reno, Nevada). But they knew they had to move on to reach the Sacramento Valley before winter, to avoid becoming trapped in the Sierra Nevada. Exhausted beyond belief, they abandoned more wagons and pressed forward on foot, only to be stunned by a major snowfall in late October. The arrival of the season's first snowstorm—one month earlier than usual—would prove to be the final nail in their collective coffin.

The party made several attempts to cross the Sierras that winter, but due to severe weather with unending snowfall, subzero temperatures, and extreme fatigue they could go no farther. They found themselves snowed in until spring. They lacked the energy to go just one more day over the summit to the friendlier side of the Sierras, where search parties could have reached them.

At Truckee Lake, the emigrants decided to set up camp and hunker down for the winter. However, in mid-December, fifteen of the strongest among them (ten men and five women) set out across the Sierras to summon help. Thirty-three days later, only seven members of the group arrived at Bear Valley, 40 miles north of Sutter's Fort, and found rescue parties about to start out. Eight of the emigrants had died along the way.

Meanwhile, in roughly constructed cabins and other shelters spread out around Truckee Lake and Alder Creek, the other members of the Donner Party waited for rescue parties, hoping that those who were sent for help had made it through. One snowstorm followed another, and hunger followed more hunger.

Unbearable months in the most deplorable conditions gave way to the unimaginable. Buried under 22 feet of snow and dying of starvation, many of the stranded emigrants were forced to cannibalize their own, living on the flesh of their dead to survive. It is difficult to imagine the horror—not only for them, but also for their family and friends back home when news of the tragic circumstances reached them.

Eventually, four separate rescue parties evacuated the emaciated survivors who had survived nine snowstorms. Tamsen had built up her daughters' strength with the arrival of new provisions and bravely sent them with the third rescue party, choosing to stay behind and comfort her elderly, dying husband. One more day would have made the difference, for the day after Tamsen's daughters left for safety, George died.

It would be another five weeks before the final rescue party arrived. By the time they reached the camp, there was only one person still alive: Louis Keseberg, a German immigrant. The leader of the rescue expedition wrote, "Mrs. Donner's body is nowhere to be seen." It was thought that Keseberg had cannibalized Tamsen Donner, and he later came to regret snide comments he had made in response to the accusation. Taunted as a man-eater until his death at an old age, Keseberg never revealed the secret of Tamsen's demise.

Fortunately, Tamsen Donner's two youngest daughters, Georgia Ann and Eliza, were eventually adopted by a Swiss couple living near Sutter's Fort. Young Frances was also adopted—by James and Margaret Reed, who had miraculously survived the harsh journey and terrible winter.

Tamsen Donner was one of the most courageous women to ever trek westward on the Oregon Trail. She was selfless and loyal to the very end. No one knows what went through her mind during those last few weeks as she strived to keep death at bay. Perhaps she recorded the details of the ordeal in the journal that she religiously kept, but that too was never found.

He Who Laughs First

• 1847 •

The rope attached to the heavy wagon was slipping through Henderson Luelling's hands, yet the burning sensation paled in comparison to the pain of the financial loss he was about to experience. With every ounce of strength he had, Luelling, dripping in perspiration, held his ground. When his heels, embedded in the earth, began to give way, though, it became apparent that he was no match for the toppling weight of his wagon. As Luelling's proposed fortune slipped out of his hands along with the rope, his wagonload of goods tumbled down a steep bank of the Snake River near the end of his journey. Drenched to the skin, Luelling awoke with a jolt and sat up in bed, relieved when he realized that it was just a nightmare plaguing him a week before his departure.

Henderson Luelling, a Quaker from Iowa, had a grand plan to transport his nursery of grafted trees from his orchard all the way to Oregon over the Oregon Trail. The recurring dream must have been his subconscious worrying about the feasibility of it all. Having packed up all that was dear to him, family included, Luelling would soon find out if he could make his fortune.

Those who had gathered to see off the Luelling clan on that spring morning of April 17, 1847, came for various reasons. Some tearfully came to bid dear friends a fond farewell; some came to wish them luck; and some came for a good laugh.

The Luelling caravan included the Luelling, Hockette, and

Fisher families. The Luelling family—Henderson, Elizabeth, and their eight children—plus their provisions, trees, and shrubs, were all packed into four wagons. The Hockette and Fisher families added another three wagons, for a total of seven wagons in the caravan.

The typical emigrant wagon was 4 feet wide and 12 feet long. However, Luelling had an especially strong wagon built to his specifications. The special "tree wagon" held two 4-foot-by-2-foot boxes that were 12 inches deep. Luelling filled these boxes with compost made of charcoal and rich Iowa soil. Then he planted 700 trees and seedlings directly in the soil.

Admittedly, attempting to transport an entire nursery's worth of trees 2,000 miles over the roughly mapped-out Oregon Trail was a bold endeavor. The "road," which had seen just a few years of overland travel, could be not only challenging but unforgiving, and no amount of determination could overcome unforeseen obstacles.

The eight Luelling children waved wildly to friends and family until their town of Salem, Iowa, was merely a speck on the horizon. The four wagons in the Luelling train seemed to be merrily bouncing along over the prairie and out of view. Ranging in height from 20 inches to 4 feet, the trees could be seen waving even more wildly than the Luelling children in the unmistakable, specially designed lead wagon crammed with hundreds of trees, bushes, and shrubs. As comical a sight as it was, Henderson Luelling had no idea that this cargo of trees dancing along in the breeze would be exactly what would ensure his family's safe passage over the Oregon Trail.

A skilled and successful nurseryman, Luelling had spent ten years grafting superior stock with his proven stock, and he knew that his nursery was superior to others. It had never occurred to Luelling to try his luck at anything else. People were beginning to settle in the Oregon country in record numbers. Luelling predicted that the homesteaders out west would be eager for sweet, delicious fruit, and he could taste a sweet, delicious profit as well. Luelling had learned that the fertile Willamette Valley soil and the climate of the Pacific Northwest would be perfect for growing fruit, especially apples. What he couldn't foretell was how interesting his traveling trees would be to the Indians he would encounter along the way.

Henderson and Elizabeth's eldest son, Alfred, a capable teen, was entrusted to drive the tree wagon and make sure the precious cargo was watered every day. It was a huge responsibility, for Henderson Luelling was about as attached to his fruit trees as he was to his children, so Alfred took the job very seriously. It was backbreaking work to water the trees and fill the extra casks, lugging bucket after bucket from the river. Alfred couldn't help but notice the Indians in the distance watching his every move as he performed the laborious task of tending to the trees.

For a while the seven-wagon Luelling caravan joined a larger wagon train, and at first everyone seemed intrigued with the traveling nursery. Soon there were accusations, though, that Luelling's slower-moving, cumbersome tree wagon was impeding the wagon train's progress. The general consensus was that it would be impossible to transport such a load clear across the Oregon Trail through the upcoming desert, mountains, and inclement weather. The presence of the Native Americans, who were clearly fascinated by Luelling's cargo, put the already-nervous emigrants on edge. Thus, the Luelling's seven-wagon caravan was left with no choice but to strike out on their own.

The unexpected tragedy of having to bury his friend, Thomas Hockette, alongside the trail was an emotional setback and immense burden for Henderson Luelling and the entire party. The obvious loss of manpower, having to care for another family, and being constantly watched were beginning to take a toll. The future of his family depended on the trees surviving, and Luelling must have begun to feel the burden as if he were pulling the tree wagon himself.

Already two cattle had been lost on the Sweetwater River; the party could not afford to lose any more. Due to an unmerciful rainstorm, twenty trees had perished before the group crossed the Platte River. Then the severe drought claimed more trees, and the roving nursery began to dwindle. The children resented having to ration their water supply to save the trees.

With too few men to stand guard, Luelling attached bells to the cattle at night so he would be alerted in case of theft. Surprisingly, though, the Indians that they encountered gave the lonely wagon train a wide berth, allowing them to pass through the Indian lands unmolested. Luelling learned that the Indians believed that the Great Spirit dwelled in trees. Indian custom even dictated that the remains of their dead be interred in the branches of trees. Here was a man crossing their land with traveling trees, and he was therefore thought to be under special protection of the Great Spirit.

It was also fortunate that the Luellings had brought along their trade wagon loaded with provisions they had hoped to use to open a store in Oregon. Though these supplies were also dwindling, the goods and trinkets served them well in dealing with the Native Americans.

Luelling wanted to reach The Dalles in Oregon, which was where the emigrants gathered to take on the rocky rapids of the Columbia River. And he wanted to get there quickly, for Elizabeth was expecting a child. Luckily, Luelling realized that the Indians presented no imminent danger, as they had kindly aided the party in the river crossings and had enjoyed peaceful exchanges. Luelling felt he must entrust to these native people the care of his wife while he worked to transport the trees in a lighter wagon with a double team of oxen. The Indians willingly transported Elizabeth, along with her eldest son and daughter, Alfred and Mary, by canoe to The Dalles to seek medical attention. Hasten as they did, nature had its way, and on the banks of the Columbia River in Oregon Territory, the Luellings' ninth child, a son, was born.

Elizabeth and her newborn, appropriately named Oregon Columbia, were then taken to The Dalles where they rested in a camp while her husband made preparations for the last leg of their journey.

The final challenge involved devising a way to safely transport the trees down the turbulent Columbia River. First Luelling saw to it that the trees were carefully uprooted and wrapped with torn canvas pieces for warmth and protection. Then he ferried them down the raging Columbia River on flatboats. It was harrowing to see the precious cargo floating on the wild and raging river. Once the flatboats careened out of control downriver. Nearby Indians in apparent awe of the floating trees rescued the wayward flatboats and pulled them to safety. Luelling was equally relieved to see his family transported safely.

Seven months to the day from his departure, Henderson Luelling and half of his stock, but all of his children, plus one, arrived in Oregon's Willamette Valley. Thanks to the aid of various Native American tribes along the Oregon Trail, the tree wagon survived its grueling cross-country trek.

Luelling's foresight in bringing the first grafted fruit orchard to Oregon would bring unprecedented success for his family. His good reputation and that of his brothers who followed (spelling their surname Lewelling) grew in proportion to the demand for his fruit trees. Over the years, hundreds of thousands of trees and shrubs from the Luelling/Lewelling nurseries and orchards spread out over Oregon, which came to be called the "Land of the Big Red Apples." The brothers extended their nurseries and orchards to California, and their fruit brought phenomenal wealth to both states.

Henderson Luelling was quoted as saying that the return for his effort was "a dollar a drop for the sweat I lost in getting the necessary water to keep them alive while we crossed the desert; and their luscious fruit repaid me many times over the jeers, ridicule, and contentions of my comrades."

In 1947 the town of Milwaukie, Oregon, held a centennial anniversary celebration of Luelling's arrival in their great state. Along with the plaque-placing ceremony, an apple pie festival touted pies made with fruit from the Luelling trees. Likewise, in a 1969 ceremony in Salem, Iowa, five trees grafted from the original ones Luelling had taken cross-country were brought back to the Midwest and were planted in front of his house, which was once associated with the Underground Railroad in Iowa. The house is now known as the Luelling Quaker Shrine, dedicated to a man whose fruit trees were the apple of his eye.

Turnarounds

• 1847 •

Columbia Lancaster, an attorney from Centerville, Michigan, had heard of "the elephant," but he certainly did not expect any confrontation with it quite so early on in his trip. More precisely, he never thought it would take him down. Yet here he was, just five days into his journey, and he was already lamenting the fact that he and his family had ever started out over the Oregon Trail. Beating himself up with regret did nothing to assuage his broken heart.

Holding the limp body of his small daughter in his arms, the distraught father fell to his knees. He laid his head on the shawl that blanketed the earthly remains of his deceased sixteen-month-old girl. His wife, Susan, was beside herself with grief as she sat kneeling at his feet, sobbing uncontrollably.

Too difficult to comprehend, it was a surreal experience for the Lancasters. Much time and energy had gone into the careful planning and preparation for their overland journey. It seemed like just yesterday that they'd gathered at Elm Grove, 20 miles west of Independence, to "jump off" (pioneer lingo for starting out on the Oregon Trail) to lands unknown.

To the best of Columbia Lancaster's recollections, the caravan had gotten as far as the Little Wakarusa River in Kansas Territory when fever claimed the life of their young daughter on May 21, 1842. The emigrants were wary of delays and had consequently planned to reserve layovers for the benefit of the whole caravan. However, in deference to Mrs. Lancaster, who had fallen ill after the death of her only child, and perhaps out of respect for her loss, the company did allow a three-day layover from May 27 through May 30. But the delay would not prove long enough to make the rest of the journey bearable for the couple that year. Eventually the grieving parents resigned themselves to returning to the Missouri/Kansas crossing and then home to Michigan. Unfortunately, their defeat was not unique.

In the earliest days of westward migration it had become painfully clear to everyone on the cross-country trek that there was one animal no emigrant wanted to see on the Oregon Trail: "the elephant." Some people ran into it head-on; some confronted it and survived; some fortunately skirted it altogether; but most assuredly every emigrant had heard of it. "Seeing the elephant" was a euphemism for facing adversity on the Trail. The well-known expression summed up all the hurdles that set up a sometimes invisible, but perceptible, blockade that prevented the overlanders from successfully crossing the Trail and reaching their destinations. The goal of every westbound traveler was to survive any and all encounters with the phantom elephant.

For some, the mythical animal reared its ugly head and took them down through disease, accident, starvation, or weather extremes. Others faced injury, thirst, or other hardships. Perhaps Columbia Lancaster had thought that the far-off land called Oregon held such promise that the risks inherent in getting there were worth it. Regardless, he was eventually forced to turn back, as were many other travelers.

A rather sizable group of emigrants came face-to-face with "the elephant" on their journeys and turned around and headed for home. Either unfortunate circumstances dictated the necessity to retreat, or the wise saw the writing on the wall and heeded the warning signs, not being willing to risk their lives for what amounted to nothing more than a chance for a better life. These emigrants were called "turnarounds." Those who chose to retrace their steps must have felt that life was not quite so bad back home after all.

Though it is impossible to get an accurate number for the returnees, the Oregon Trail saw its fair share of them, for many an emigrant journal made mention of it. Historian John D. Unruh Jr. estimates that there were hundreds, if not thousands, of returnees in 1849, 1850, and 1852 alone.

Some turnarounds, also called go-backs, made it only as far as the jumping-off towns along the Missouri River before they changed their minds about the trip. Perhaps the outfitting cost alone was prohibitive for the would-be overlanders. Maybe the stories that the merchants in town repeated about the cross-country trek were overwhelming to those who weren't completely sold on the idea to begin with. Some emigrants traveled for only several hundred miles before they'd had enough; others ventured out quite far on the Oregon Trail before they did an about-face.

Clearly, every returnee had a point when too much was too much. The difference was where they drew the line beyond which they would not go. Mary Ellen Todd, a relative of Abraham Lincoln's wife, Mary Todd, left Arkansas for Oregon in 1852. She claimed that ninety-six wagons in her hundred-wagon caravan turned around and headed home after traveling a considerable distance on the trail. Another report stated that an emigrant woman buried her husband past Salt Lake City, Utah, in 1852 and made the return trip 1,000 miles from whence she had come.

In 1850 Seth Lewelling met a 300-wagon caravan retreating to the jumping-off town of St. Joseph, Missouri. Whether due to poor planning, theft, or loss, they had insufficient provisions to sustain them clear across the continent. That year the drought, coupled with high Trail traffic, forced numerous turnarounds. Many companies competed for the same limited supply of grass for their stock. Emigrant Dabney T. Carr witnessed a party who started out too early, could not find sufficient grass, and resorted to feeding their own food to the animals to sustain them on the trip home.

The year 1852 was a particularly bad one for the dreaded cholera, an often-fatal intestinal disease. Emigrants overusing unclean campsites with contaminated water sources allowed the cholera to reach epidemic proportions. A bride from Elkhart, Indiana, Jane D. Kellogg, found her cross-country honeymoon excursion tinged with sadness. She wrote in June of 1852 that emigrants could be seen burying their loved ones both day and night, with multiple gravesites next to each other. That same year more than 600 miles out, just past Chimney Rock, E. S. Carter witnessed what was left of a large caravan heading east, devastated by cholera. Apparently they had seen enough of "the elephant" to last them a lifetime.

Death of family members and those critical to seeing the caravan through demoralized some emigrant parties so much that "home" was the only direction in which they headed. In 1852 a young married couple, Ezra and Eliza Jane Meeker, reportedly met eleven wagons whose women drivers were returning home since all the men in their company had died.

What fragmented many caravans were company disputes. Some quarrels were legitimate disagreements over routes and safety issues, but others were nothing more than power struggles and bickering. One emigrant spoke of so much discontent among parties along the Sweetwater River one-third of the way along the Oregon Trail (in present-day Wyoming) that it seemed as if no one at all got along.

The turnarounds heading east surely must have felt like fish swimming upstream as the plethora of emigrants continued to stream westward. It may have been intimidating for those heading out to hear stories of dire consequences of "the elephant" ahead on the trail from these backtrackers. Perhaps the westbound emigrants overlooked this as they eagerly gleaned as much information as possible from the go-backs. Pummeled with inquiries about trail conditions, available water, wood, and grass, as well as unforeseen dangers ahead, most returnees were forthcoming with advice and even good-naturedly transported letters back home for the westward emigrants.

Travel over the Oregon Trail presented the challenge of a lifetime, especially in the early 1840s when the Trail was not well defined. Forts had not yet been established where provisions could be purchased or stock exchanged for fresh oxen. It took great courage and determination to head off into uncharted territory with limited information about what to expect. The reluctant traveler surely had to wonder just when the journey would end. Adult emigrants trudging along on foot constantly encouraged their children to press forward through conditions most cannot even imagine.

What may seem even more unfathomable is that the turnarounds who made it safely back home sometimes considered heading out on the Oregon Trail again one day. Columbia Lancaster and his wife did just that. After the death of their baby daughter and their retreat to Centerville, Michigan, they started out again—five years later—on March 4, 1847.

The determined Lancasters were better prepared this time, with much advice acquired from newspaper accounts and letters from experienced travelers. The now took along five yoke of oxen and a specially designed larger wagon with the amenities of a cook stove and spring bed for ease of travel. Along with seventy wagons in their company, Columbia Lancaster and his wife and new child completed their overland journey in six months. On this, their second attempt to master the Oregon Trail, the only "elephant" they encountered was "mountain fever," which, fortunately, they survived. At long last their dream came to fruition when they pulled into Oregon City on September 15, 1847.

In the succeeding years Columbia Lancaster became a prominent member of western society. He and his wife Susan settled near the mouth of the Lewis River in Oregon Territory, which eventually became the state of Washington. Columbia

Lancaster was appointed associate justice of the supreme court under the provisional government. He was later elected as a Democrat to the thirty-third Congress for the Territory of Washington.The Lancasters were also blessed with two daughters, Sarah and Hannah. In the end, their long trek, great sacrifice and loss, and perseverance led them to a new and fruitful life at the end of the Oregon Trail.

Patience of a Saint

•1847•

This truly had been the worst day in Samuel Markham's life. From a distance he could see the fiery glow intermixed with the thick black smoke rising up into the air, and he just knew that he owned the problem. Turning around, the emotionally exhausted Markham mustered his remaining strength and ran to see what more could possibly have gone wrong.

Earlier in the day his pregnant wife, Elizabeth Markham, had been fed up with all the vexations that come along with Trail life and simply refused to go one step farther. She forbade her children to even think of getting into their wagon that morning. For three hours Samuel Markham had tried to convince his wife to join the caravan and continue onward, but it was to no avail. Elizabeth was not going anywhere.

Some of the company had moved on, leaving Samuel Markham to deal with his difficult wife and the difficult situation in which he had found himself. After all attempts to coax her to continue had failed, Adam Polk (a relative), Cornelius Smith, and a Mr. Kimble physically removed the young children from their stationary post and put them into the covered wagon. The emigrants who had stayed behind looked to one another in disbelief as the remainder of their caravan was now pulling out, leaving Mrs. Markham sitting smack-dab in the middle of the Oregon Trail.

After some time, Elizabeth supposedly dusted herself off and headed back in the opposite direction on the Trail. Once out of sight, however, she took a side route and overtook the wagon train. In the interim, Mr. Markham had sent their fifteen-year-old son, John, back to retrieve a horse he had inadvertently left in camp. In seeing Elizabeth return to the caravan, and in thinking that she had come to her senses, Samuel Markham asked his wife if she had come across their son. As he waited for her reply, a demented look came across his wife's face. Her eyes, devoid of expression, stared straight ahead. Then she turned her head, fixed her eyes upon her husband, and replied, "Yes, I picked up a stone and knocked out his brains." In shock, Mr. Markham took off to find his son.

It was when he was searching for the boy that he had noticed the fire and the smoke. Sure enough, one of his own wagons was going up in flames. In a state of frenzy, the stunned travelers threw buckets of sand and dirt onto the fire. Blankets were sacrificed to smother the flames, and precious water was used to douse the engulfed wagon until it was completely extinguished. The singed edges of the burnt canvas top flapped in the wind and the wagon's arched wooden bows were laid bare, as if a charred and broken skeleton was exposed for all to see. Markham's goods wagon, stocked with the necessary supplies to ensure his family's survival on the Oregon Trail, had almost been totally destroyed.

Amid the pandemonium and confusion stood the motionless, expressionless Elizabeth Markham. Elizabeth turned toward her husband and gave him a smug and defiant look, and the bewildered man knew that it was none other than she who had set the family wagon on fire. As if it were too preposterous to be true, Samuel at first walked around his wife with his head cocked to the side, staring at her in utter disbelief. Then a seething anger started to slowly rise in him. It was as if the fury began in his toes and rose up through his body until the wrath defined and consumed him.

Approximately 15,000 emigrants had made the pilgrimage westward over the first six years that the Oregon Trail had been officially "open." Over time, it had become painfully clear that not everyone was up to the challenge of life on the Trail. In an attempt to portray what Trail life was really like, newspaper editors published excerpts from overland diaries, journals, and letters. The public devoured them. No matter how these first-person accounts and guidebooks tried to prepare the travelers, though, it was impossible to accurately capture life on the Trail. Words may have been able to describe the experiences, but they failed miserably in depicting the accompanying emotions.

It is not known whether Elizabeth Markham willingly chose to uproot her life and travel in adverse conditions for seven months over the Oregon Trail. Few were the wives who rebelled against their husbands' decisions. Nonetheless, the Markhams had bid farewell to their family and friends, never to see their home again. Emotionally equipped or not, Elizabeth had prepared provisions for the trip for herself, her husband, and their five children: Daniel, twenty-three; John, fifteen; Warden, twelve; Henry, six; and Mary, three. There were 140 emigrants in their caravan journeying from the Missouri River to Oregon. There may have been other women who, like Elizabeth, were expecting a child while traveling 2,000 miles on foot across the continent.

The rugged land with its continual challenges had forced the emigrants to see that their lives were held in a precarious balance. They knew that the scale could tip either way. The precipitous cliffs could cause their wagon to topple over, and the desert with its stifling dust could get a stranglehold on their parched throats and take them down. The tumultuous thunderstorms with their riveting rain fell from violent night skies that were split apart by lightning bolts. Pummeled mercilessly, everyone was left drenched to the skin and aching with fever and cold.

It didn't end there. All the travelers suffered from hardship and hunger. Meat, flour, and beans were traded with Indians, only to be desperately needed later. The chaotic and riotous river crossings were nothing short of nerve-racking. In crossing the Snake River, the Markham's caravan saw a man drown, leaving behind a wife and six children. When a majority of the work oxen turned up missing, a search ensued that resulted in a man accidentally shooting and killing himself. He also left a wife and six children uncared for.

No one knows just what put Elizabeth Markham over the edge on the day when she refused to continue her trip. Perhaps she envisioned herself widowed as well along the Oregon Trail, left with the daunting task of completing the perilous journey without a husband. Maybe she could not bear the thought of anyone in her family dying along the Trail.

Most likely it was the culmination of one provocation after another, for the overland trek had provided more than its fair share of vexations. Whatever the reason, September 15, 1847, Elizabeth Markham cracked under the strain of it all.

In actuality, Elizabeth had never laid a hand on their son John. She claimed to have done so only to get a rise out of her husband. Ill-advised or not, she had taken the opportunity to make her point.

Remarkably, the Markhams did complete their journey over the Oregon Trail. Mrs. Markham gave birth in Oregon, and she aptly named the baby Columbia after the Columbia River. In this tradition she joined many overland women who named their offspring after the terrain near which they were born. Samuel and Elizabeth Markham must have eventually made up, for a seventh child was born to them two years later. Edwin Markham went on to become a widely acclaimed poet. However, soon after Edwin's birth, Mr. Markham left for California and never returned. Certainly any turbulent marriage would be hard-pressed to survive the difficulties of settling a new country; the Markhams were just one unfortunate example. Seven years later, Elizabeth Markham took her family to California, where she remarried, though that husband also left her.

The Oregon Trail doled out its share of challenges that no one but the travelers themselves could truly comprehend.

Everyone who set out on the journey had his share of courage, determination, and stamina, but not everyone was equipped with enough fortitude. Fear of the unknown and the irrational-yet-understandable terror of not knowing when the Trail would claim its next victim got the best of some early pioneers. Those who traveled in the Markhams' caravan in 1847 clearly saw what could happen if one didn't possess the necessary coping skills. Perhaps it gave them incentive to hold it all together when they saw poor Elizabeth Markham fall apart.

The following poem by Elizabeth Markham is one of several published in the *Oregon Spectator,* in Oregon City, on June 15, 1848, the year following the family's arrival in the West. It depicts opposing views of the institution of marriage. (Elizabeth's note to the reader stated, "To advocate the ladies' cause, you will read the first and third, second and fourth lines together.") The reader is left wondering whether Elizabeth had a sense of humor or if her poem expressed her true feelings about married life.

A Contrast on Matrimony

The man must lead a happy life,
Free from matrimonial chains,
Who is directed by a wife
Is sure to suffer for his pains.

Adam could find no solid peace,
When Eve was given for a mate,
Until he saw a woman's face
Adam was in a happy state.

In all the female face, appear
Hypocrisy, deceit, and pride;
Truth, darling of a heart sincere,
Ne'er known in woman to reside.

What tongue is able to unfold
The falsehoods that in woman dwell;
The worth in woman we behold,
Is almost imperceptible.

Cursed be the foolish man, I say,
Who changes from his singleness;
Who will not yield to woman's sway,
Is sure of perfect blessedness.

Up, Up, and Away

•1849•

The Oregon Trail and the California Trail, which were one and the same for nearly 1,000 miles, were seeing a lot of traffic by the late 1840s. As the number of emigrants heading west increased, trail-travel enthusiasm set many an entrepreneurial mind to work. Budding inventors looked to devise alternate modes of transportation to cut the time needed to cross the country.

The inventor of the "wind wagon," a man named Frederick "Wind Wagon" Thomas, felt sure that he could cash in if only he could fine-tune his contraption. This combination wagon/sailboat attained 15 miles per hour, a marked increase over the 2 miles per hour of the average covered wagon. The only drawback was that this new mode of transportation didn't handle rocks or crevices well. On one test drive, the crew had to "jump ship" just before it crashed into a gully. Though Thomas had begun work on his idea three years before the Gold Rush, thirteen years later it still wasn't quite up to speed.

A creative fellow named Rufus K. Porter came up with an idea that was truly unique for its time. Porter was an ingenious inventor who envisioned westward travel not by land or by sea, but by air. Porter's idea was for a balloon-powered airship. This was to be no small balloon, but one large enough to carry many passengers, along with their luggage, clear across the continent. A determined Porter, working tirelessly to prove the feasibility of his airship, faced some tough opposition.

While Porter's more progressive contemporaries could conceptualize directed balloon flight, many thought the practicality of such travel to the West Coast was preposterous. Porter's critics claimed that he had crossed the line from sane to insane. One critic wrote, "Though every man of sense is or ought to be aware of the impossibility of steering a balloon or any other aerial machine, yet it seems it has been found, in New York, a fellow who was knave or fool enough to advertise, for exhibition, a Flying Machine." Another wrote, "We have heard of nothing more ridiculous."

Nineteenth-century America was a time of progressive thinking, and Rufus K. Porter was a major contributor whose practical inventions saved time and labor. He had invented an air pump, a prefabricated movable house, a life preserver, a revolutionary rifle, a fire alarm, and many other interesting contraptions. He drew up plans for an automobile and an elevated railroad. He made loads of other mechanical drawings and produced models for machines that came to be mass-produced in the twentieth century. He was truly adept at visualizing possibilities.

Porter's proposed "travelling balloon," or "flying machine," was his true love. In 1834 he had published his plans for his flying apparatus. By 1841 he had a machine-driven model. The spindle-shaped craft was to be 350 feet long and 35 feet in diameter. It was propeller-driven by a steam engine and used charcoal as its fuel. There was a device on board that produced hydrogen gas to inflate the balloon. Suspended underneath was a salon (passenger/cargo area) attached by cords or wires. A ball-and-socket control and both vertical and horizontal rudders allowed the airship to be easily directed and to have the ability to land and lift off. The craft was even buoyant for the unlikely event of a water landing. And the passengers' safety was assured—the balloon came with parachutes, and potential passengers were informed that the baggage "would eventually all come to land in due time" should they abandon the airship.

Porter had tried to imagine and prepare for all possible situations that could occur while flying.

In 1847 Porter exhibited a small working model of his airship in New York. Timed precisely for the onslaught of pioneers heading west, another exhibit appeared in 1849, along with an advertisement: "The Practicality of Traveling Pleasantly and Safely from New York to California in Three Days. Wine Included." Rufus Porter would have been more than willing to fly the emigrants to any destination. For $50, fifty to one hundred passengers would be able to travel at the breathtaking speed of 60 to 100 miles per hour. This superseded any other mode of transportation of the day. But rather than enticing the public, this seemingly ludicrous claim further solidified the critics' opinion of Porter.

A determined Porter spoke at public gatherings and wowed audiences when he demonstrated the workability of his "aeroport." Without complication, the model airship simply rose above everyone's heads and circled the room. One can only imagine the gaping mouths and looks of disbelief on the faces of the critics. Perhaps Porter felt vindicated as the critics, ready with their disparaging quips, were suddenly silenced. Traveling over the Oregon Trail held new promise.

Porter engaged more than 200 passengers to sign up for the experience of air travel across the continent. He even petitioned Congress to finance this potential for rapid cross-country travel and mail delivery.

Forced to concentrate on raising the necessary funds and to lead public opinion, Porter set to work. His twenty-five years as an itinerant painter, along with the money he gained from his inventions (some were never patented), brought in little revenue. In the 1840s he published and edited the *New York Mechanic, American Mechanic,* and *Scientific American,* writing prolifically to drum up interest in his airship.

Finally, in 1852 construction of Porter's aeroport—the culmination of his life's work—began. Unfortunately, a severe storm damaged the craft's framework when it was near completion. Next the canvas began to disintegrate due to the type of varnish used, and then vandals slashed the balloon.

Still, Porter would not give up. He formed the Aerial Navigation Company and issued stock. He offered half of his patent claims and agreed to accept a low profit margin for the promotion and funding of his invention. Even with all that, he did not have enough takers to raise the necessary $15,000. Without the requisite funds, Porter knew that his idea would never fly, and sadly, it never did.

When Porter died in 1884 at age ninety-three, his aeroport had yet to be launched. Yet Porter's fifty years of research on aerial locomotion was a significant contribution to flight research. He conceived of his revolutionary airship thirty-five years before Orville and Wilbur Wright were even born.

Considering Porter's contributions to art, science, and journalism, one would think that this was a man whose ideas should have been taken more seriously. After all, the *Scientific American,* which he founded in 1845, was one of the most important journals of its day—and is one of the two oldest periodicals in circulation more than 150 years later.

But Rufus Porter was apparently not destined to be recognized in his own time. His hometown of West Boxford, Massachusetts, omitted his name from the "Distinguished and Professional Natives" chapter when *The History of Boxford* was published in 1880. Even in 1945, on the one-hundredth anniversary of *Scientific American,* Rufus K. Porter was never mentioned as a founder or editor.

In 1913, nineteen years after his death, the *New York Sun* said that Porter was the "father of the dirigible airship," for his knowledge of aerial navigation far surpassed that of his contemporaries. Porter himself had correctly prophesied that an aerial locomotive would one day be the "general instrument of transportation of merchandise, as well as mail and passengers, throughout the world."

Rufus K. Porter's power-driven working models of his airship were flown successfully. If the necessary funding had been secured, his airship might have become a reality, too. There is no telling how many emigrants' trips across the Oregon Trail might have been safer and faster as a result.

Unexpected Luxury

•1849•

By 1849 emigrants were setting off in record numbers to travel over the Oregon Trail. In this year of westward migration, most had some idea of what they were getting into, though no one could fully comprehend all the risks involved. The unexpected obstacles and the innumerable vexations were perhaps balanced by some pleasant surprises that caught everyone off guard. One such surprise occurred in central Wyoming in the middle of desertlike conditions. For Alonzo Delano, a relative of President Franklin Delano Roosevelt, it couldn't have come at a better time.

Alonzo Delano's doctor had advised the young bachelor that a change of climate, fresh air, and the exercise provided by a trip across the plains would improve his vigor and restore his health. Judging by his symptoms, it's likely that Delano was suffering from "consumption," better known today as "tuberculosis." Delano therefore bid his parents farewell in Aurora, New York, and then left his residence in Ottawa, Illinois, and set out to travel the Oregon Trail for 1,000 miles. He would then head off in the direction of the California gold fields to find his fortune.

Delano took the Illinois River to St. Louis, Missouri, and the Missouri River to St. Joseph, one of the "jumping-off" towns that had sprung up along the frontier. There he outfitted himself for the journey ahead. On April 19 his seventeen-wagon caravan, under the leadership of Jesse Greene, pulled out of St. Joseph on what was to be a four-and-a-half-month excursion.

The men divided into groups of seven to a wagon; many of the wagons were reserved for provisions. They were fifty men, a "mighty army on the march," as Delano described the throngs of westbound emigrants.

There was a saying on the trail that "to *know* one's neighbors, they must be seen on the plains," for the stress of life on the trail could bring out the best and the worst in anyone.

After the first 300 miles of generally level plains, the Trail turned rough and rocky. There were long stretches without water. Dangerous river crossings challenged the emigrants, and violent thunderstorms stampeded their livestock. Compounding the emigrants' frustration was the remarkable clearness in the atmosphere that made it difficult to accurately judge the distance from landmarks. It was no wonder that by the time their caravan was making its way through the desert, the men's tolerance was at low ebb. The blinding and choking dust that sat 6 inches atop the clay soil had the consistency of flour. When the wind kicked up, it rose to an impenetrable, fine cloud so thick that Delano could not see 10 feet in front of himself to the lead oxen. The dust seeped into everything; even the food was covered with an ashen hue. To keep tempers from boiling over, the men agreed to rotate the order of the wagons. That way everyone could enjoy some relief at the coveted front spot of the train, where the dust was less thick.

The 110-degree desert temperature caused the wood to dry, and the wagon wheels repeatedly shrank from their iron rims. Frequent stops to build sagebrush fires to repair the wheels in the oppressive heat began to take a toll.

On June 26, some 60 miles past Independence Rock, approaching the Sweetwater River, they reached a large number of teams waiting to cross the river. Rather than wait for hours to make the crossing, they decided to take an old, sandy, hard road, which sent their wagon train on an 8-mile stretch under the hot sun with no water.

Delano impulsively jumped on a horse named Old Shab. He took off for the snowy mountain peaks looming in the distance, hoping to bring back water. After an afternoon of reprieve and refreshment in the cool foothills, he realized that it was getting late and prepared to head back for camp. While taking a different route back, Delano came to a rapidly running brook. He was eager to join up with the caravan to see if they too had come upon the same brook. Delano galloped on, following the brook down to within a mile of the trail, where the water mysteriously sank into the ground and seemed to disappear.

When Delano caught up to the caravan hours later, he learned that the day had continued to be oppressively hot and dry and that no one had seen any sign of any water whatsoever. It was then that Delano noticed that at the point where he overtook the train there was a soggy, spongy morass to the right of the road. This low, swamplike marsh resembled a hay meadow and was about 1 mile long and half a mile wide. Delano thought that this surely must be where the water he'd seen earlier had ended up.

By this time, the thirst-crazed emigrants had barely any strength left from trudging along in the heat all day. They must have looked at Alonzo Delano as if he had lost his mind when he suggested that they all get their shovels and get to work digging for water. Some of the men took spades and began to dig furiously. About 1 foot from the surface they struck not water, but something hard. Incredibly, upon further excavation the hard object was found to be a layer of ice 5 to 6 inches thick. Chipping out a large chunk, the travelers found ice-cold water beneath.

The emigrants stared in disbelief. Just moments before, the chances of getting a delicious ice-cold drink of water on a 110-degree summer day in the middle of an apparent desert would have seemed nonexistent. Delano's discovery seemed nothing short of miraculous.

Delano correctly surmised that the thick growth of high grass prevented the sun from melting the ice that had formed during the previous winter. At the high altitude of 6,000 feet above sea level, the water in the sagging valley floor collected and froze during the winter. It was insulated by the thick, heavy, peatlike turf atop it.

The emigrants used axes and spades to cut through the sodlike peat to reach the ice and water. In some places the water above the ice was tainted with alkali, which was why the grass there was discolored. Beneath the ice slabs, though, the water was especially clean and fresh. This natural icehouse was a curiosity to all, and it quickly quenched their aching, parched throats. At 862 miles from civilization, it seemed to be an answer to a prayer afforded the emigrants at the precise moment it was needed.

The word spread to caravans behind that up ahead on the right side of the road there was an icy spring, or ice slough, offering unsurpassed refreshment. Eager not only for drink but to rid themselves of the paste of dust and sweat caked on their skin, the emigrants went into the bog en masse, laughing and dancing as if they didn't have a care in the world. The ice chunks even provided the rare treat of ice-cold lemonade for the evening meal that day.

Years later, in 1862, an angry and disappointed emigrant who'd had no luck locating the coveted ice felt he had been deceived. He asserted that the ice slough was a "cold-blooded romance." Many pleasantly surprised emigrants continued to harvest the previous winter's ice, however, nearly depleting its supply over the years. Today the ice slough, found 15 miles west of Jeffrey City, Wyoming, is still there. On rare occasions the persistent and patient digger can harvest a thin sheet of ice under the smelly peat, though the days of finding huge, thick ice chunks are gone. The peat now works in reverse, acting as an insulator and keeping the winter chill from reaching the trapped water.

Alonzo Delano's cross-country trek did improve his health and he did end up in California. After mining for a while, he prospered as a merchant in San Francisco. He also became a noted author, railing against incorrect information regarding Trail travel. With all that the emigrants had to deal with, Delano thought that at the very least they should be armed with accurate facts. The journal that Delano kept is hailed as an overland classic and was one of the earliest published.

Against All Odds

•1850•

It was one of those delightfully cool, crisp autumn mornings that offered up a day full of possibilities. Hiram S. Young had a spring in his step as he hurried along to the slave auction block on East Lexington Avenue in Independence, Missouri. As he passed by his shop on North Liberty Street, he paused for a minute to look up at the hand-carved sign hanging above. "Hiram Young—Manufacturer of Ox Yokes and Bows." Yes, life was good! He lingered for a moment, proud of his accomplishment. There was no time to waste, however, as he always made it his practice to arrive early to look over the slaves before the auction began.

Young had ambivalent feelings about the auctions. No matter how many slaves he bought, he was always disappointed that he couldn't buy them all. He searched for the men who looked determined and hard-working and showed promise. When it came time for the auction to begin, the shocked looks on the faces of those who had gathered never escaped Young. It must have been quite a surprise to see a black man buying slaves! It was Hiram Young's intention to eventually free the slaves he bought. They could purchase their freedom with money they earned by working for him.

Hiram Young was born a slave himself on a plantation in Hawkins County, Tennessee, around 1815. At age thirty-two he had convinced an abolitionist, George Young (whose surname he took), to purchase him so that he could work out his freedom for an agreed-upon sum. Hiram and his wife and new master then moved to Missouri, where Hiram continued to whittle ax handles and ox yokes on the side to earn the necessary $900. It took several years to earn his freedom, though: After realizing Hiram's value, his owner had raised the price of his freedom to $1,500. In addition, Hiram purchased the freedom of his wife, Matilda. This ensured that any children born to the couple would be free too; according to the law of the day, children born to black couples took the status of the mother. With their freedom attained, Young and his wife moved to Liberty, Missouri, in 1847. In 1850 they relocated 7 miles south to Independence with their six-month-old daughter, Amanda Jane. There they were three of forty-one free blacks.

By this time Young had saved some money and he invested in land grants. The federal government was giving away free land out west in Oregon Territory. People only needed to reside upon these donation land claims and cultivate the land. After a few years they then became the rightful owners and could sell the land for a profit if they chose.

Young, either alone or with his family, may have traveled the Oregon Trail and lived in Oregon for three years. There is an entry for a Hiram S. Young on claim 4937 in Polk County, Oregon, for October 1, 1850. Or perhaps he paid someone else to sit on his claim. Regardless, three years later the claim was settled, on March 30, 1853. It is thought that Young might have made some of his money on land speculation, which he then invested in his business.

Using his carpentry skills, Young set out to establish himself as a wagonmaker and whittler of ax handles and ox yokes. The same skills that he used to purchase his freedom would now be put to use to carve out a new life for his family.

Independence was the county seat of Jackson County, Missouri. It was an economic center of trade, having long served the trade industry over the Santa Fe Trail. The Santa Fe

Trail, which opened up in 1821, ran from Independence, Missouri, to Santa Fe, Mexico (now New Mexico). Freight caravans serviced the many trade opportunities between American and Mexican merchants for sixty years. Hiram's wagons and yokes had been primarily used for government freight transport of mail between Independence and the lands in the West. In the 1840s when Independence began offering goods and services to emigrants traveling over the Oregon and California Trails, it became a major outfitting town. Realizing how fortunate he was to have his business in such a prime location, Young also began servicing the westbound emigrants in the early 1850s. With his expertise and good business sense, his business thrived.

Hiram Young believed that the color of one's skin had nothing to do with one's abilities, and he was determined to let nothing stand in his way. He was one of only eleven wagon and carriage makers in Jackson County and the largest in Independence. The quality and craftsmanship of his covered wagons and ox bows were indisputable and his work was highly sought-after. His well-built wagons went for $160 to $250, and he sold ox yokes for $2.25 apiece. His reputation and the quality of his work had made his business incredibly lucrative.

By 1860 Young and his employees were producing between 800 and 900 wagons and thousands of ox yokes each year. The wagons were branded with "Hiram Young & Company," and Young carved the initials of each purchaser below a wagon's brand, adding to the prestige. It was said of Young: ". . . one Negro man who had purchased his freedom from his master became the proprietor of an ox yoke establishment . . . of the very best class of yokes, that were to be found in all the country. . . ."

In railing against the injustice of slavery, Young purchased as many slaves as he could afford to employ in his shop and his farm, allowing all of them to earn money to buy freedom for themselves and their families. He then used the money paid to him to purchase additional slaves, who could work out their freedom as well. By all accounts Young was recognized as one of Independence's wealthiest entrepreneurs. He described himself as "a colored man of means." The 1860 census listed Hiram, age forty-six, Matilda, age thirty, and their daughter, Amanda Jane, age fifteen, as mulattoes (persons of mixed race). By 1860 the free-black population had expanded and Hiram Young was one of seventy free blacks living in Independence; he was also one of the richest men in the country, black or white. He was said to be fifty-six times wealthier than the average person. His personal property was listed at $20,000, his real estate at $36,000, and he was the owner of three slaves. Just east of Independence, Hiram and Matilda lived in their well-appointed house in Little Blue Valley, which included a 480-acre farm where Young employed fifty to sixty men. At his shop in town, he employed twenty men.

However, Missouri at that time was pro-slavery and not always accepting of free blacks and mulattoes residing in their state. The free black man had to find where he fit in society. It is unclear whether the white citizens of Independence accepted Young and his family, but they certainly respected his work. He lived during a time when tensions between blacks and whites were high, and the slavery issue, being hotly debated, was building to a crescendo that would be played out in the Civil War. It was a time of great opportunity and economic reward, but it was rocked with discontent.

For his family's safety, Young moved them to Fort Leavenworth, Kansas, during the Civil War, where he worked for the U.S. Army. Returning to Independence after the war, Young found that the Union troops had confiscated his farm and destroyed his shop. He filed a lawsuit against the government and set up a new business in the interim. Anticipating that the railroads would supersede the need for wagons, Young built and operated a successful planing mill. He cut timber needed for railway ties and shaved lumber into flat boards that would be used to construct buildings all along the railroad routes. Here he did blacksmithing and made tool handles in addition to wagons.

When Young died in 1882 at age 67, his lawsuit had not been resolved. Twenty-five years later, in 1907, the courts ruled that the government owed Young nothing for the Union Army's damages and consumption of his goods and property.

Due to Hiram Young's determination to better his situation in life, the lives of his family and many others were forever changed. Transitioning from bondage to freedom, this resolute pioneer craftsman successfully started two businesses and beat the odds against him. He supported schools for black children in Independence, though he himself could not read or write. He funded his daughter's education at Oberlin College in Ohio. His daughter later taught in and was principal of a school in Independence named after Young. Hiram Young was an accomplished, dynamic man, a success story born out of sheer determination, and an inspiration to many. And he was a man who made the most out of living and working at the very start of the Oregon Trail.

The Marriage Bed

•1850•

Running out to the dilapidated barn, the young woman pushed open the squeaky door and snatched up one of the unsuspecting cats, hiding it in her apron. When no one was looking, the young woman tore across the yard with the captive struggling to free itself from the tangles of its entrapment. She burst through the front door, her eyes twinkling with excitement, as she greeted the circle of girls waiting for her in the front room of her farmhouse in Des Moines, Iowa.

The nimble fingers that had diligently stitched the patchwork quilt for months had put down their needles and thread. The fifteen pairs of hands held tightly to the edges of the star-patterned, multi-colored masterpiece. The quilt had finally been removed from its frame and was now unfolded and held taut, ready and waiting. The young woman quickly tossed the cat onto the newly finished quilt and it bounced into the air several times, to peals of laughter and giggles. As the cat bounded toward one of the girls, everyone screamed. The lucky recipient of the cat nearly fainted. She would be the next to marry.

Rebecca Nutting was well aware of such romantic superstitions, which were used to divine the future, and she wasn't alone in wondering who her husband would be. Most girls felt that they were destined to marry, and foretelling each other's prospective mates through rituals such as the cat on the quilt was a popular pastime. To Rebecca, any of the common practices (reading tea leaves, looking for signs in the moon and the stars, or reading the reflection in standing water) would suffice as well as the cat on the quilt.

Many teen girls who started out over the Oregon Trail carried these superstitions with them. Their heads were full of dreams about what the future held. Fourteen-year-old Rebecca Nutting was bursting with excitement as her family and the Hickmans, who had been friends for years, began their overland journey. Rebecca's head was filled with romantic notions, and she just couldn't quite grow up fast enough. Many girls her age were nearly married, and fifteen seemed a good age to settle down. Though personal items were limited to make room for necessary provisions in a traveling wagon, nearly every unmarried girl packed something for her hope chest. It wasn't just to have a sentimental reminder of home. Every prospective bride wanted to have something special for her wedding day, such as a pair of candlesticks, a family bible, a treasured china figurine, or even some lace that could be used to decorate a wedding dress. The opportunity for purchasing finery in the unsettled land out west was virtually nonexistent.

Most girls on the frontier were married between the ages of fifteen and twenty. Men were usually about five years older. Most men spent some years surveying job prospects before settling down. Both sexes considered marriage desirable, for it allowed for the apportioning of necessary chores. Girls, while usually free to marry whomever they wished, looked for a dependable mate for life. When getting hitched, love was a bonus.

For most young people, life on the trail provided the perfect setting for courtship and blossoming love. Young Rebecca Nutting, ever poetic, wanted nothing more than to see a trailside wedding. She took one look around at all the youngsters in the company of twenty-one wagons in their caravan and felt sure that love was in the air. In fact, one young man in particular had taken a fancy to Rebecca's dear friend, Catherine Hickman.

For Rebecca, Catherine, and other lighthearted, happy youths, the trek over the Oregon Trail was seen as a "continuous picnic" and "excitement was plentiful." Perhaps the married folks let them enjoy their carefree days, which seemed destined not to last very long. One scarcely went from being a child to having a child, for after courtship and marriage, children usually followed quickly.

Blissfully unaware of how quickly their lives would change, most young men and women on the Trail just looked forward to the day's end, when there would be time to make merry. The division of labor that generally separated them fell by the wayside at night, when there was time for social interaction. After the evening meal, while the adults met to make plans for the next day's drive, the younger set could entertain themselves with "concerts," or dances, on the prairie. The married folk joined in the music and dancing around the evening campfires, but generally they retired early, leaving plenty of time for the youngsters to fan the flames of romance. One evening, Rebecca sat with her friend Catherine, listening to the fiddler play "Turkey in the Straw." Rebecca felt a rush of excitement when Catherine whispered to her that she had accepted the hand of David Parks, who had hired on to help Mr. Nutting see the wagon train through. The two star-struck youngsters became engaged around the time that they crossed the Missouri River. Not wanting to wait until the end of the Trail, the young lovers decided to marry then and there on the prairie. Mr. Nutting set out back to nearby Kanesville to fetch a preacher, and the young couple was united in matrimony on the plains with the backdrop of the horizon as their church.

Catherine and David's wedding on May 21 offered the romance that young Rebecca was desperately hoping for. In quick fashion there was a wedding wreath to make from woven wildflowers for Catherine's head, and food to prepare for the wedding feast. Luckily, their caravan had not been out on the Oregon Trail all that long when Cupid's arrow had struck, so there were plenty of special provisions with which to make the wedding "banquet" out on the grassy plains.

Most wedding celebrations lasted into the wee hours. After an evening of dancing and merriment, glowing newlyweds took to their covered wagon to retire for the evening. A lucky bride was one who had a feather comforter to lay over the bulky wagonload of provisions to make her marriage bed. Couples tried to find comfort and some semblance of privacy where they could in the cramped quarters of the caravan of many wagons.

But under the canopy of evening stars that May night, the young Mr. and Mrs. David Parks's peaceful dreams of a romantic evening were boldly interrupted. In the black of the night, a scurrying group of men with hushed but chuckling voices ran to pick up the tongue of the newlyweds' wagon. An equal number of women likewise pushed from behind, dragging the wagon a half-mile out on the prairie.

Everyone in the camp who had come to join in the revelry serenaded the unsuspecting couple. The noise was enough to wake the dead. Young and old alike banged together any available metal objects, shook chains, shot off guns, and played crazy music on makeshift instruments. They were joined by a chorus of manmade barnyard animal sounds, singing, laughter, and shouts of joy. Everyone attempted to make as much noise as possible. After the merrymakers disbanded, the new Mr. and Mrs. Parks were left on their own to enjoy the rest of their wedding night. Such "shivarees" were common on the frontier. To Rebecca Nutting, nothing could have been more romantic! The blushing couple walked back into camp the next morning among the good wishes and cheers from their friends and traveling companions, ready to begin their new life together.

Perhaps Rebecca Nutting had stitched her hopes and dreams for the future into her own quilt when she sat among her friends in the sewing circle back home in Des Moines, Iowa. The marriage she had longed for did occur when she was almost sixteen, not out on the prairie, but at the Trail's end. She was happily married for seventeen years and had nine children. Her second marriage, which brought another child, was an unhappy one and lasted only briefly. Rebecca Nutting fondly referred to her journey over the Trail as "Oh, those happy days."

Etched in Stone

•1852•

The stars were just starting to twinkle as the music from someone's fiddle began. Amid the laughter and chatter, the dancing had begun. It was nearly impossible to concentrate on the task at hand with all these distractions but, as always, work came before play. Seventeen-year-old Jenny Scott dutifully sat by the light of the evening campfire, recording the day's events as her father admonished her to "keep the diary correct." Out of the nine Scott children, Jenny had been chosen as the designated scribe on her family's journey over the Oregon Trail. Night after night, no matter how tired she was, Jenny would sit precariously perched on the front wheel of their covered wagon, with journal and pen balanced on her lap.

To Jenny and her siblings, most days seemed no different from the day before. The young people searched for ways to pass the time on the Trail. At first they found taking turns riding in the covered wagon fun, but they soon tired of the bone-jarring jostling and chose to walk beside the wagon as the miles of their journey stretched on. Similarly, the novelty of recording the day's events had worn off when there was nothing new to record.

However, June turned out to be a month to remember. Everyone had been happy to see Chimney Rock—one of the most recognizable landmarks along the Oregon Trail—come into view on June 14. The emigrants were even more elated to reach Independence Rock two weeks later, on June 29.

Independence Rock, located 830 miles down the "road" from Independence, Missouri, was one of the most famous and eagerly anticipated Trail landmarks. Upon spotting the immense formation of granite rock on the horizon, the emigrants began to cheer and chant. This chorus soon gave way to the sound of the hastening of the beasts of burden carrying the pioneers to the spot where many caravans were gathered. No one was prepared for either how massive or how isolated Independence Rock was. The oval stone outcropping looked like a beached whale on the open plain rather than the beginning of the Rocky Mountains.

Situated on the Sweetwater River, Independence Rock provided the perfect setting for a layover. Everyone had heard the story of the monolith being christened "Independence Rock" by celebrated fur trader William Sublette, who had passed by on his way to a fur-trading rendezvous on July 4, 1830. Even more popular were the tales of finding familiar names left on the rock, such as those of well-known explorers, leaders, and trailblazers. Young people hoped to locate names like J. C. Frémont, Brigham Young, and Kit Carson. A highlight of the Oregon Trail trip for the youngsters was finding a place to add their names to the throngs of others inscribed on the rock. Some youths, with their competitive nature, wanted to put their names higher than anyone else. Jenny just hoped to leave her mark somewhere on this public register for all to see.

The youngsters of Jenny's party and those of others who camped there set about clambering over the great rock. Plans for inscribing their names had been conceived long before the trip began, and the concoctions they had brought along to daub their names were many. They had an assortment of mixtures: paint, axle grease, India rubber, chalklike substances, and combinations of gunpowder, tar, and buffalo grease. A determined few attempted to carve or chisel their names or initials for a longer-lasting impression.

It took a full ten minutes to scale the rock to its pinnacle, where a minimal amount of soil allowed for the growth of some scanty shrubs and a lone dwarf pine. From there one could take in the panoramic view or sketch the surroundings. All the way around the base of Independence Rock, which felt like a mile in circumference, were the names or initials of emigrants scrawled as high as one could climb—up to 6 or 8 feet high in some spots, and much higher in others. Climbers had to be careful to skirt the rattlesnakes nestled in the bed of weeds around the base of the rock, but this didn't faze the boys and girls who were busy devising ways to ascend to seemingly unreachable heights to find blank spots where they could write their names. Those who could not scale the giant rock enlisted older boys or men to do the engraving for them, some for a monetary reward.

Reading the names left behind by fellow emigrants was almost as exciting as making your own mark on the rock. It was reported that a cavelike depression in the southeast corner sported the best inscriptions, as it was most protected from the elements. The earliest signature located belonged to M. K. Hugh, who carved his name in 1824. The best thrill of all, though, was to discover the name of someone dear who had reached this landmark before you. To touch the impression made by a friend or a loved one—and just to know that they had made it this far—was cause for great joy.

Jenny's sisters, Fanny, Maggie, and Kate Scott, were just as eager as the others to find any famous names and to inscribe their own names on the wall. However, locating a clear spot in which to do so was no small task. The girls were a bit encumbered in their climbing by their long dresses, but they were not the least bit discouraged. At first they made steady progress and had ascended approximately 30 feet, but then the weather took a turn for the worse. A windstorm arose out of nowhere, and the girls were caught in heavy, pelting hail. They were forced to abandon their plan and seek cover.

Not realizing that they had been out much longer than they had planned, Jenny, with Fanny, Maggie, and Kate in tow, reluctantly headed back. They were understandably disappointed as they saw their wagon train pulling out of camp. That meant that they would never get a chance to carve or paint their names. (The captain had decided to leave without the girls to teach them a lesson not to stray so far from the wagon train.) The girls ran after the caravan and overtook the last wagon before it crossed the river, avoiding a waist-deep wade through the water. Besides being teased about almost being left behind, the girls were saddened that they had not been able to add their names to the greatest collection of autographs along the Oregon Trail. Jenny would have to wait for a later date to leave her mark in the world.

Later that night Jenny Scott sat and recorded her impressions of the day that had been so full of excitement. The emigrants thought that Independence Rock seemed to cover ten acres, though in actuality it covered roughly half that number. They estimated its size, which was 650 yards long and nearly 220 feet high at one end. Upon closer scrutiny one could see that the hard stone mass was made up of separate large sections compacted together into a giant mound. It was remarkable that anyone succeeded in scaling the smooth granite rock at all. Jenny sat near the campfire late into the night, recording all that she could remember about the impressive landmark.

During the Scotts' six-month trek along the Oregon Trail, Jenny dutifully fulfilled her role as scribe as well as other inherited responsibilities. She bore her share of heartache along the trail, for in between Chimney Rock and Independence Rock her frail, hard-working mother succumbed to cholera. Jenny mournfully recorded the death of her mother early in their journey, as well as the death of her three-year-old brother two months later. Still grieving, the Scotts pulled into the Willamette Valley on September 28. With virtually no energy left to begin carving a life out of the wilderness, Jenny began her teaching career. She was determined to succeed, knowing that her mother had sacrificed her own life to better those of her children.

When Jenny married at age eighteen, she saw firsthand how difficult life could be for women. In addition to carrying out back-breaking farm work, being a homemaker, and raising her children, Jenny had to provide free meals for neighboring bachelor men who had no one to cook for them. This exhausting regimen made Jenny begin to resent that her life was turning out to be just like her mother's, that of a "general pioneer drudge." After her husband, Ben Duniway, suffered an accident, Jenny was forced to support him and their six children. She taught school, operated a women's dormitory, opened a millinery shop, and edited a newspaper she had founded.

Seeing how little control women had over their own lives gave Jenny the incentive to do something about it. Jenny, born Abigail Jane Scott, rallied against the injustices that women faced, and she decided that women's lot in life would never change until they had the right to vote. As an adult, Abigail Scott Duniway dedicated her life to blazing a new trail. She promoted women's issues as an author, as a journalist for her weekly newspaper, as a public speaker, and as a campaigner pioneering for women's rights to vote and to own property. She joined forces with Susan B. Anthony as one of the country's leading suffragettes (women who support the right of women to vote).

At age seventy-eight, Abigail Scott Duniway saw Oregon grant women the right to vote. She died five years before the passage of the Nineteenth Amendment to the Constitution, which gave all women the right to vote. The Jenny Scott who, as a child, missed her opportunity to leave her name along the Oregon Trail during her family's crossing went on to leave an imprint much more lofty and lasting than any image painted or etched on Independence Rock.

You Can Run, But You Cannot Hide

• 1852 •

A billowing cloud of dust hung overhead, making it hard to tell just how many wagons had pulled up. Each succeeding wagon train that arrived on the chaotic scene found it more difficult than the last to ascertain what all the commotion was about. Hundreds of loose cattle were braying, an unknown number of creaking wagons were trying to reposition themselves, and men who couldn't be seen, but only heard, were shouting directions amid the noise and confusion. Even so, some information filtered down. Details were sketchy, but apparently a posse was being formed. A search was under way for a dozen or so good horsemen from the assembled wagon trains. The volunteer riders were needed to apprehend two men who had recently absconded from camp after committing an atrocity.

Guns in hand, the posse took off from LaBonte Creek Crossing (in present-day southeastern Wyoming) in hot pursuit. The culprits were a nineteen-year-old man named Lafayette Tate, along with his teen brother. Both men were from Jackson County, Missouri. The duo had murdered a fellow emigrant in their wagon train, disarmed the onlookers, then fled.

While the posse was tracking down the villains, the shell-shocked emigrants who had witnessed the cold-blooded murder recounted the ordeal for those who had gathered afterward.

According to the emigrants in the wagon train, they had just crossed gulleys and ravines in the scorching heat and plodded through the thick, fine sands of the Platte River Valley, so they were glad to stop and refresh themselves and their stock at Warm Springs. Then, while the wagon train was camped just 2½ miles southeast of LaBonte Creek Crossing, the unspeakable had happened.

The emigrants' caravan was a rather large one, headed by a Mr. Brown. Brown had decided to stay behind with a drove of cattle in need of more feed and water. He had asked a man in his train, named Miller, to take charge of leading the caravan in his absence. Apparently Miller's temporary position of leadership irritated the Tate brothers, who were also members of the caravan. The Tates had an obvious dislike for Miller. In deference to Mrs. Brown, who had wished to lay over after a while and wait for her husband to catch up, Miller ordered the caravan to halt. The Tates wanted neither to stop nor to take orders from Miller, and a heated exchange ensued. Miller felt that the Tate brothers' foul language defied his authority, and he struck one of the brothers with his whip. Rather than quelling the confrontation, Lafayette Tate became enraged by seeing his brother struck, so he took matters into his own hands. In a fit of rage, Lafayette Tate plunged his knife into Miller's back between the shoulder blades. As Miller fell, Lafayette slit his throat as well.

Feeling that they were above the law, the brazen teen brothers quickly planned their escape. They robbed the dead man of his knife and pistol and disarmed the onlookers who had been too shocked to take any decisive action. They threatened the life of one emigrant and chased him as he ran to another wagon train for cover. Then the brothers Tate headed out to take the California road rather than continuing on to Oregon, thinking that no one would give up precious travel time to leave the trail and apprehend them.

By the time the gruesome story had been told several times and the details patched together, some caravans had moved on to distance themselves from such vile behavior and other trains had arrived to whom the incident was relayed once more. By the next day, the triumphant posse rode back into camp with the accused Tate brothers in protective custody.

A defiant Lafayette Tate boldly claimed that there was no law on the plains. He insisted that if he was to be tried, he should be sent back to civilized society. West of the Missouri River was unsettled country with no organized civil government, but disciplinary action was enforced along the Oregon Trail. Usually each caravan wrote up their own constitution before heading out on the Trail, and all emigrants were expected to abide by it.

The general consensus was that crimes committed on the plains should be tried on the plains. If the accused were found guilty, punishment should be exacted on the plains. Therefore, in the Tate case, the law of self-preservation manifested itself in the convening of a "high court." The wisest and most trusted elder males were pressed into action, having been chosen as judge and jury from the 200 wagons gathered in the vicinity that day. A self-appointed "lawyer" was assigned to each side, and after the witnesses testified, the accused had his say.

After a fair trial, Lafayette Tate was found guilty of murder in the first degree. After the verdict was read, the sentence was pronounced. Once a decision was handed down, all agreed to see that justice was carried out. Given time to make his peace, the indifferent man had half an hour to himself, during which he showed no remorse. Near midnight on June 15, 1852, Lafayette Tate was hanged from a cottonwood tree alongside the creek. His brother, who vowed he would seek revenge on the jury, was whipped for his involvement in the crime and was later repentant.

The trial and execution of Lafayette Tate was just one of many that occurred on the Oregon Trail. When extended periods of stress put emigrants near the breaking point, situations that got out of control made tempers flare, and unchecked words and deeds sometimes led to inconceivable action. While a headstone marked the name and date of a grave's occupant, it became common practice along the Oregon Trail for criminals' offenses also to be exposed for all to see. On a wooden grave marker, the dastardly deed and the punishment doled out were written down. Emigrants hoped that these placards would either teach a lesson or warn would-be villains passing by.

The crime, the trial, the hanging, and the burial of Lafayette Tate had all occurred within a twenty-four-hour period. Justice was swift on the Oregon Trail so it would serve as a deterrent. Arbitration helped to settle disagreements and minor offenses. Stealing was punishable by whipping with an ox lash, but capital punishment was exacted for murder. It was a sobering experience for the emigrants in the caravans involved. Those who chanced to pass by a few weeks later saw the gruesome effect of Lafayette Tate's disturbed grave, which had been dug intentionally shallow so that the wolves had easy access to it.

A Kindness Returned

•1852•

Dr. William F. Alexander, looking rather disheveled, left the livery. Carrying a cumbersome canvas sack of sawdust on his shoulder, he headed down the street. He opened the door of his apothecary shop, paying no attention to those around him who noticed that he was peppered in sawdust himself. Stepping inside, he let the sack fall heavily to the floor. Then he sat down in the corner, packing his stock of medical supplies in the old but sturdy trunk he had recently purchased. He had vials of morphine for pain, hartshorn for snakebite, citric acid for scurvy, and quinine for malaria, as well as tincture of camphor, castor oil, laudanum, calomel, a box of physicking pills, peppermint essence, rum, brandy, rattlewood tea, mustard, and also opium and whiskey, which served as a general cure-all. After shaking the last bit of sawdust from the sack into the well-packed trunk, the doctor closed the lid tightly and locked it. Placing the key in his vest pocket, he felt his heart beating fast. All that he was worth was now packed in that trunk, along with his dreams and aspirations. He had spent his life's savings outfitting himself for the overland journey on which he was about to embark.

It was the spring of 1852 and the optimistic, and rather naïve, Dr. Alexander was heading west over the Oregon Trail. He had heard that the fertile Willamette Valley was starting to fill up with settlers from the East, and that spoke to the young man who had spent several years serving as a country doctor.

Settlers would need medical attention in their new towns, and Dr. Alexander hoped to fill that need. A mere 2,000-mile journey across the continent, and he could set up his own practice. What Dr. Alexander did not anticipate, however, was that his skills would be called upon long before he reached Oregon.

Dr. Alexander was not particular about which wagon train he hooked up with. He soon discovered that he had his choice, as any caravan willingly accepted a doctor among its number. As his chosen caravan proceeded, they found that the first third of the Oregon Trail was geographically the easiest section with the flat plains offering a manageable terrain. It was also very scenic: gently rolling plains with head-high waving grass and abundant wildflowers. The slow-moving but sometimes deceiving Platte River was a reliable pathway from Nebraska to Wyoming. All the overlanders came to use it—which was precisely the problem.

The year 1852 just happened to be the peak year of travel on the Oregon Trail. That year alone, about 70,000 emigrants journeyed through the same area. Though the emigrants wouldn't have known it at the time, sanitation and health are directly related. Thus the first section of the Oregon Trail also held the distinction of being the most disease-ridden. Campsites there were overused, and contact with contaminated water was inevitable. Cholera, a bacterial infection that spreads through the use of contaminated water, was at epidemic proportions that year. This intestinal infection causes symptoms such as diarrhea, vomiting, and leg cramps, which can lead to severe dehydration and death. Fortunately, Dr. Alexander was more than willing to serve all who needed him. He traveled on horseback at all hours of the night as emigrants sought him out. He rode through all kinds of foul weather and adverse conditions, often between caravans that were 30 or 40 miles apart. The trials, the fatigue, and the exposure that had been part of his job description as a country doctor back home ended up being good training ground for the Oregon Trail.

A hundred miles or so past Fort Laramie, the altitude generally killed the cholera germs. But about 250 miles west of Fort Laramie, news reached the doctor that the dreaded cholera had struck once again. Onto his horse Dr. Alexander climbed, literally racing against death. He had seen firsthand how cholera had raged through wagon trains, sometimes claiming entire families. Its sudden onset and quick progression were usually deadly. To battle cholera, a doctor could administer a compound of barks and roots or give liberal doses of brandy, mustard, laudanum, and rattlewood tea. Often, though, those who contracted the disease in the morning found their way to the grave by evening.

Race as he did, Dr. Alexander was too late to save the patient that he was brought to see this time. Joseph Newman, head of the Newman wagon train from Terre Haute, Indiana, had been riding his horse just that morning and yet was dead by nightfall. The poor young Mrs. Annie Newman had been the next victim, but luckily the doctor had arrived in time to administer some medicine. Annie Newman was exhausted, but still fighting for her life. At times she was coherent enough to realize the predicament she was in without the aid of her husband to see them through. She was terribly worried about her two stepsons, who were only ten and twelve years old. Dr. Alexander did all that he could for his patient and sat vigil with her through the night as both nursemaid and doctor. He wiped her forehead and patted her hand as he patiently listened to her ramble on. For hours she drifted in and out of consciousness. In bits and pieces, the doctor learned that the couple had intended to open a general store with a stock of dry goods that they had brought along with them. At morning's light the weakened Mrs. Newman showed signs of recovering. Though Dr. Alexander was reluctant to leave her side, he knew that his services would soon be called upon elsewhere. Confirming that Mrs. Newman's hired men would oversee her recovery and take her family through to Oregon, the good doctor wearily headed back to his own wagon train.

For some reason Dr. Alexander could not get the sweet young mother out of his mind. She had evoked a special tenderness in him. He assumed that he had left her in good hands. However, in truth, the Newmans' hard-hearted and disloyal hired hands cruelly took off with Joseph Newman's strongest oxen and stole all the family's goods. The scoundrels took all the wagons except the one in which Mrs. Newman lay recovering, leaving her and the boys to fend for themselves.

Meanwhile, Dr. Alexander's thoughts had turned to where he was needed next. The situation in which he had found himself was dire. More than 5,000 emigrants died from cholera in 1852 alone. A single overlander counted 401 fresh grave sites along the way. Another emigrant recorded in a diary: "The Sign for a new grave was to See their feet with old Shoes or boots on Sticking up through the Sand and at other places you saw the old hat & dusty garments that had been thrown away & quite a number had been So lightly Covered with Sand or Sod the Kiotes had drawn them partly out & Eat of the Carcase this is a common occurrence on the plain."

There were so many sick and suffering along the Oregon Trail that year that the generous Dr. Alexander found himself continually dipping into the medical supplies he had so carefully packed for his new practice in Oregon.

On the last section of the trail, Dr. Alexander saw many cases of scurvy caused by eating too few fruits and vegetables for too long a time. There were other illnesses to deal with as well, such as measles, mumps, smallpox, pneumonia, dysentery, tuberculosis—commonly referred to as "consumption"—and diarrhea. Needless to say, the good doctor's vision of a romantic, fun-filled adventure disappeared as quickly as his supply of medicines.

By the end of the seven-month journey, when Dr. Alexander finally arrived in Oregon, the well-packed trunk of vials, pills, powders, and ointments that constituted his medicine chest was all but empty. His kindness and generosity had forced the young doctor to put his dream on hold for a while.

Dr. Alexander had never forgotten the young Mrs. Newman, whom he had comforted through a night of cholera. In Oregon, he inquired about her fate. He was saddened to learn that she and her stepsons had been robbed and deserted, but was very relieved that another wagon train had compassionately taken them safely to Oregon.

In Linn County, Dr. Alexander found a position teaching school, settled on a humble claim, and was married, all within four months of his arrival. With whom did he share his life? None other than the beautiful and sweet Annie Newman, the young widow whose life he had saved along the Platte River on the Oregon Trail. He sought her out to ask for her hand, and she accepted. After years of saving, the doctor replenished his "medical trunk" and opened a practice, serving as a doctor for more than thirty years in western Oregon. The Alexanders' house was more like a hospital than a home, and both Dr. and Mrs. Alexander came to be known for the kindness and generosity that they showered upon others.

Bubble Up

•1852•

It was the Fourth of July, and back in Cambridge, Ohio, there would be grand marching bands, a town parade, and spectacular fireworks to celebrate the anniversary of the nation's birth. But the only parade Dr. John Hudson Wyman found himself in was that of a slow-moving caravan of a few traveling companions, trudging across the country. Celebrating Independence Day on the Oregon Trail could never compare to how the doctor's friends were celebrating back in the States. However, Wyman and his caravan did find some excitement that day.

As if out of nowhere, a strange sound up ahead on the Trail interrupted the otherwise routine but pleasant morning. If John Wyman and the others hadn't known better, they would have sworn that they were back in St. Joseph on the Missouri River, getting ready to disembark from one of the grand steamships to begin their overland journey. Several emigrants ran toward the riverbank to see what the commotion was. Even the oxen appeared eager to investigate the diversion and willingly picked up their pace to join in the inquiry. What man and beast found through an opening in the rocky ground was a 3-foot-tall tower of white spray that was jetting upward with considerable energy. The sound of a forced gurgle and hissing of gas generated from underground water pressure accompanied the spurting water. The explosive burst of noisy steam was unmistakable, and the emigrants quickly came to understand why the guidebook mentioned that Steamboat Springs was in this area.

The Oregon Trail passed along the Bear River in present-day southeastern Idaho. Located near the north bend of the river called Soda Creek was an area referred to as Soda Springs. This was a famous landmark along the Oregon Trail. Steamboat Springs was just one of the many natural wonders found there. The natural soda springs bubbled up through soil rich with calcium carbonate and iron, shooting various geysers into the air. Fountains of water spurted upward. From other openings in the earth, gaseous steam jets issued forth, creating a misty white cloud of water vapor. There were thousands of small springs for a quarter mile on Soda Creek between Steamboat Springs and the drinkable Soda Springs.

Dr. Wyman's first view of the mineral springs was upon ground composed of white limelike schist rock. The springs that percolated through the ground left sediments of mineral deposits several feet high next to the pools of bubbling water. The doctor later recorded in his diary, "These are the greatest Natural curiosities that I ever saw."

After traveling through the arid, sandy Wyoming prairie, the thirsty emigrants were overjoyed to have come across the fresh water. They welcomed the opportunity to replenish their supply for the trip ahead, and every barrel, gourd, and jug was filled to capacity. Though the water was certainly refreshing, the emigrants disagreed in their opinion of it as a beverage. While some found the bubbly, clear water quite pleasant, most seemed to prefer it sweetened. As one man duly noted, "The water with a little sugar is very good drink, but by itself is very poor soda." The soda water was an effervescent water charged under pressure with carbon dioxide. It was similar to today's mineral water and had an iron aftertaste.

The fact that the day was the Fourth of July was as good an excuse as any to be in a celebratory mood. One particular group of men had a special fondness for the plentiful drink they'd discovered. Presumably desperate to entertain themselves, they had a rather jovial time at the aptly named Beer

Springs, where the non-alcoholic soda water produced an especially noticeable foam. The men filled their tin cups to the brim and soon raised their frothy mugs to toast and joke in a mock-inebriated state of stupor.

These springs seemed like a gift from Mother Nature—and a timely one indeed for emigrants who had just walked approximately 1,000 miles. The travelers were eager to bathe and rid themselves of the buildup from their daily trek. Even their dusty brown clothes had lost all hint of color long ago and needed a good washing. Wyman noticed that there were ten or twelve springs in an area of less than half a square mile. The springs resembled boiling kettles sunken in the ground. The water temperature varied; Wyman estimated the temperature of one thermal spring to be 98 degrees Fahrenheit. The variety of openings in the ground allowed ample room for bathing in the hot, soothing water. With separate pools of cool drinking water nearby, the emigrants felt revitalized. There was even lush grass nearby, courtesy of the naturally irrigated land. The overtaxed oxen needed a reprieve as much as the emigrants did, and the beasts grazed nonstop for hours.

The emigrants were not the only ones to benefit from the springs. Nearby, Wyman noticed a trading shack operated by some settlers who had taken advantage of the location's obvious appeal to weary emigrants.

There were also Indian wigwams in the area. The Indians who lived near the Wasatch Mountain Range called the area "Tosoiba, Land of Sparkling Waters," and they had been coming to the area for generations. The Indians believed that the waters offered a remedy for many ailments and held secret healing powers. Bathing in the springs was believed to have a soothing effect on the body and spirit.

In addition to the novelty of the hot springs and their value as a bathing spot, Soda Springs was an important landmark for another reason. Just a few miles west, at Sheep Rock Point, lay the junction of the Oregon and California Trails.

Here the emigrants had to bid farewell if friends chose different paths to follow their dreams. The left fork took travelers over the Hudspeth Cutoff and on to the California Trail. The right fork was the main Oregon Trail, which continued on to Fort Hall and along the Snake River to the Columbia River in Oregon.

As much as John Hudson Wyman and his friends reveled in the reprieve that their rest stop offered on that day, their journey was far from over. Wyman and his friends broke from the main trail just past Sheep Rock Point and headed for Sacramento.

At Octagon Spring Park in the town of Soda Springs, Idaho, a renovated octagonal 1890s kiosk shelters a carbon-rich spring once used by the emigrants on the Oregon Trail. Most of the springs that made up the Soda Springs complex have dried up. Unfortunately, Steamboat Springs and Beer Springs, often mentioned in emigrant diaries and journals, are both under the water of the Alexander Reservoir.

Today people still come from far and wide to visit Hooper Springs, which is 2 miles north of Soda Springs. Once known for its medicinal qualities, the water from these springs was sold nationally from 1882 to 1956. Hooper Springs, offering free, clear, sparkling soda water for anyone who wants to dip a cup into the spring, is the only sizable spring that served the pioneers that is still in existence today. An eight-sided open wall kiosk with a roof encloses the spring. Locals say that the clear, cold sparkling water is an "acquired taste." People either love it or hate it.

Just Around the River's Bend

• 1853 •

The monotonous prairie terrain had been nothing short of maddening for the twenty-six-year-old Celinda Hines, a native New Yorker who had expected anything but unvarying scenery for weeks on end. Celinda was making the long and arduous overland crossing with her family. As they all came to see, the Oregon Trail revealed its secrets gradually over the course of the continent. It was August when Celinda's caravan came upon Snake River Canyon, in present-day south-central Idaho. Celinda was about to see some of the Trail's most impressive sights.

As Celinda's wagon train followed the Snake River down through the mammoth cleft in the earth called the Snake River Canyon, the region exploded with wonders. The Snake River, now at its lowest elevation, meandered through the base of the canyon. The majestic walls towering overhead made the wagon train seem miniature, and the travelers making their way through the bowels of the earth felt rather insignificant. In trying to take it all in, Celinda slowly turned in a circle with up-lifted eyes. This gave her a panoramic view from the perspective of an ant.

As the sun filtered down, the dusty rays lighted a path for the emigrants who ambled along. Stopping suddenly in her tracks, Celinda felt the ground beneath her feet shudder. She cocked her head to one side and listened intently. She detected the echo of a familiar sound. After a moment she broke from her concentrated trance, and a faint smile began to form around the corners of her mouth. The smile slowly grew into a mischievous grin. Experience had told her what the trembling ground underfoot was, and the dull roar of thunder in the distance suddenly made it all clear.

Raising her dusty brown skirt above her ankles, Celinda quickened her pace to a near run and worked her way up to the head of the wagon train. This, she had to see. Within minutes the crushing sound and the rising mist let her know that she had reached her destination. As her eyes gradually rose up the craggy sides of the canyon walls, the other travelers closed in behind her and took in the same spectacular scene.

Bursting out from the walls of the canyon high above them was a series of cascading waterfalls. Not one, but thousands of waterfalls pouring from the porous canyon walls. A collective gasp ensued from each group of awestruck emigrants as they arrived at the falls. Humbled by the majesty of it all, the travelers stood there, staring in disbelief.

The gushing waterfalls, too numerous to count, came out of the sides of the canyon walls, not from any body of water overhead. Though it seemed impossible, there appeared to be no river feeding them. Fifty miles of desert land extended beyond the rim of the canyon.

One outpouring of water descended from the north side of the cliffs, about 200 feet up. Another waterfall cascaded for some distance at an angle over a large protruding escarpment before it fell. As the sun shone through, its lacelike shadow created the illusion of a veil before disappearing into the rocks below. A most-welcome spray of mist fell gently upon the emigrants, who stood with uplifted arms.

Midway up the towering walls, a giant waterfall spewed out of the side of the canyon. The mesmerized emigrants had all seen large rivers before, but never a vertical one. Some falls sprang forward from roughly the same height, but others haphazardly gushed forth from all points, uniting into one body of crystal-clear water below the bluffs.

It didn't take much to amuse the trail-weary emigrants. For many, the falling mist aroused a hidden, jovial self. Some individuals felt compelled to dance a jig or sing a song in the delicious white spray. It appeared that Nature had indeed been saving its grandest of exhibitions until this junction of the Trail, and such scenery more than made up for the long stretches of unvarying terrain.

Those who journeyed over the Oregon Trail had no way of knowing then that the disappearing Lost River of eastern Idaho joined with the underground waters in the area, where together they seeped down into the porous lava rock bed. After completing a 100-mile underground journey, the water reemerged through the larger openings in the porous lava bluffs that made up the canyon walls and issued forth in sporadic fashion as waterfalls. The emigrants on the Oregon Trail aptly named the seemingly infinite falls Thousand Springs.

In the Snake River Canyon, south of what is now the town of Hagerman in south-central Idaho along Highway 30, the modern wayfarer can still enjoy a glimpse of what Thousand Springs used to be like. Though roughly 80 percent of the waters have been harnessed by hydroelectric power plants, the remaining waterfalls are still impressive. The Lost River still gushes out of the canyon walls in spectacular patterns along Thousand Springs Scenic Byway, giving a hint of what once captivated travelers on the Oregon Trail.

Then and Now

•1853•

When the decision to go "up and over" or "find a way around" was put to a vote, the outcome was almost always unanimous. For the emigrants, the thought of retracing their steps to avoid the obstacle before them (named, with understatement, the "Big Hill") was inconceivable. One might as well have suggested that the entire wagon train turn right around and head back home 1,000 miles to where they had "jumped off" from on a site along the Missouri River.

Henry Allyn, who had left Fulton County, Illinois, on March 28, had set his sights on reaching the much-heralded Oregon. He was now confirming what he had learned long ago; the overland trek was not a trip for the fainthearted. Time and again Allyn's 1853 caravan was faced with challenges along the Oregon Trail. Today, standing directly before his wagon train, blocking their path to Oregon, was one of the steepest hills any of the travelers had ever seen. Allyn wondered just how many emigrants before him had survived Big Hill intact.

At first the narrow path Henry Allyn took wound its way gradually up the steep ravine. But even as the emigrants struggled up that quarter-mile incline, the one-mile ascent rose straight up in front of them—and it seemed nearly impossible that these wagons would be able to make the climb. Brakes like those on the typical covered wagon could not prevent the wheels from sliding backward down the hill as the oxen and horses struggled to pull them upward. Allyn and the others were resigned to using whatever materials were available to keep the wagons moving uphill. Stones, logs, and chains were utilized, and ropes were attached to every live body, both man and beast. Hoisting the 3,000-pound wagons was backbreaking work, to say the least. Most of the emigrants preferred to climb the hill on foot rather than ride in a wagon that felt as if it was ready to topple backward at any moment. There were no words, at least none that could be repeated in polite conversation, to explain the emigrants' frustration with the hill.

With extraordinary effort, Allyn's caravan successfully hauled their wagons up the near-vertical ascent, but getting up the hill was only part of the struggle. They were left with no option but to descend on the other side. The question was how to do it. Upon reaching the summit, Allyn looked straight down at the death-defying slope they now had to tackle. Below them beckoned a lush, beautiful valley known as the Clover Creek encampment. Great Bear Lake glistened far to the south with its silvery sheen. But the steep hill would be just as treacherous on the downhill side as it was on the ascent.

Allyn could easily see that Big Hill was scarred with evidence of previous unsuccessful descents. It would take some ingenuity for his caravan members to prevent such a collision and to resist being prematurely lured to their deaths. Allyn and the other emigrants mustered their energy and began painstakingly lowering their wagons down the hillside, trying to navigate it with a horizontal crisscross pattern. One woman who had begun the descent down Big Hill by sitting in the wagon seat with her legs braced against the wagon box found herself standing straight up as her wagon miraculously made it down the steep incline in one piece. Others weren't as lucky, and the horrendous sound of a wagon tumbling end over end demonstrated the powers of gravity. Even if no life was lost, a crash was tragic if a wagon was left beyond repair, for the families would then have to carry on without one.

Allyn managed to take his wagon down using ropes and chains around every available tree stump and boulder. It was a slow, arduous process that left him totally exhausted.

Conquering Big Hill on the Oregon Trail was not only an accomplishment; it was also an important milestone for Allyn's caravan. The Clover Creek encampment that they had reached was the first campsite on the western side of the Continental Divide. It marked the halfway point along the Oregon Trail.

After surviving Big Hill, crippled wagons and all, the emigrants needed to survey the damage before getting to work rebuilding, repairing axles, and gathering scattered provisions. The last half of the Oregon Trail was still ahead, but the Clover Creek encampment was a peaceful and tranquil stopover. Its beauty and lushness, with Silver Creek and the abundant green grass, must have seemed like a slice of heaven. The emigrants rested their animals, replenished their water supply, and took advantage of the opportunity to wash and bathe. Here the weary travelers could actually relax and rejuvenate themselves before carrying on.

Contemporary wayfarers still pass through the Clover Creek encampment, located in the town of Montpelier in southeastern Idaho, looking to soak up a bit of history. Entries from emigrant journals and diaries bear witness that the Clover Creek encampment was a layover that everyone enjoyed. The residents of Montpelier, in recognizing the importance of the Oregon Trail passing through their town, chose to preserve this important landmark. The National Oregon/California Trail Center, an interactive living history museum, was designed and built upon the exact location of the Clover Creek encampment. Interpreters in period costumes reenact what life was like here when the emigrants came upon this section of the Oregon Trail. The same soil that Henry Allyn and the other emigrants trod upon was set aside during excavation of the center and replaced upon its completion in an attempt to keep the Clover Creek encampment authentic.

Reenacting the pioneers' stopovers at the Clover Creek encampment in the mid-1800s helps us understand their quest. Entries from journals kept by Allyn and other pioneers give us a feel for all the trials, vexations, and joys that emigrants experienced as they followed the Oregon Trail across the country. These were people whose courage was tested and whose hardships and heartaches were real.

The High Price of Steaks

•1854•

Hans Jensen Hals, Christian J. Larson, and Hans Monson were far from their homeland in Denmark. The long, turbulent journey across the Atlantic Ocean was only the first third of their journey. After Stage Two, where the men traveled overland to Westport Landing (present-day Kansas City, Missouri), their seventy-three-wagon caravan began the last leg of the pilgrimage: 1,300 miles over the Oregon Trail.

The Utah-bound Danish wagon train that included Hals, Larson, and Monson was following the stream of emigrants along the Platte River, the best natural path west. They were one of the few Mormon companies that chose to travel on the south bank of the North Platte River, which was heavily traveled by "gentile," or non-Mormon, emigrants. The group of Mormon travelers tried to keep to themselves, but it soon became clear that there were many people sharing the same land. When they were 8 miles east of Fort Laramie, they came across an Indian camp on the north side of the Oregon Trail with 450 lodges. One thousand Miniconjou Sioux were encamped on that site.

The Indians were camped in the vicinity of a trading post. There the Sioux were awaiting the distribution of the annuity (annual payment of money and/or goods) due to them from the U.S. government. This was the U.S. government's attempt to appease the Native Americans. The practice of offering the Indians new land or payment in exchange for yielding to the whites encroaching upon their lands had begun in the mid-1800s. Initially the Indians had no idea that the emigrants traveling through their country were just a small fraction of those who were to come. But the white people came in record numbers. They brought with them diseases for which the Indians had no resistance; they claimed land that did not belong to them; and they killed off entire buffalo herds, which diminished the Indians' food supply. Thus, to temper their anger and resentment at losing their ancestral lands, the Indians, hungry and out of provisions, had come to collect the annuities owed them.

Trying to keep its distance, the Mormon wagon train ambled along the bank of the North Platte River. While one of their group was contending with a lame cow at the rear of the column, something startled the animals. The lame cow and one of Monson's cows wandered away from the caravan and into the nearby Indian camp.

The stray cows coming into their midst seemed quite fortuitous to the Sioux, and one of the young braves acted upon his hunger and shot at the cows. One cow was wounded and made its way back to the Danish emigrants' cow column, but the other was captured, butchered, and enjoyed by some of the Indians in the camp.

Hans Monson's injured cow, which returned to the Mormon wagon train across the river, was promptly butchered and was likewise eaten, as there was no saving the animal. Christian Larson, designated chaplain and accountant for the wagon train, recorded the loss and noted that their company made no attempt to reclaim the other cow, as the emigrants were fearful of the large band of Sioux. Sadly, this seemingly harmless interaction with the Indians and the cows was to touch off a series of tragic events.

Upon reaching Fort Laramie, 8 miles up the Oregon Trail, the Danish captain of the Mormon company reported the incident, perhaps lodging a complaint. The report fell on the ears of the military personnel stationed at the fort, who decided to take action.

The mission of the military was to protect emigrants on the Oregon Trail, and some officers stationed there believed in harsh punishment for all Indian infractions. The officers were still smoldering over an altercation with the Sioux the previous year, concerning the use of a North Platte River ferryboat. That incident had aggravated the already-tense relations between the Sioux and the U.S. military.

The same officers involved in the ferryboat debacle were the ones who decided to take action for the deaths of the two cows from the Mormon wagon train. Brevet Second Lieutenant John L. Grattan and the Sixth Infantry were sent to the Sioux Indian camp to arrest the culprit who had shot at the cows.

The overzealous, young, and inexperienced lieutenant was all-too-eager to demonstrate the strength of the U.S. military. Dragging along his three-pound cannon, twenty-eight soldiers, and his drunken French-Canadian interpreter, Auguste Lucien, Grattan boldly marched into the Indian camp in search of the offender. The lieutenant insisted that the four assembled chiefs surrender the brave who had shot the cows, but the chiefs refused. Instead the Indians offered a horse as repayment for the cows, but their generous offer was not accepted.

As Grattan and the Sioux chief faced one another, each sticking firmly to his ground, 500 warriors encircled them. In a show of force, Grattan unwisely directed his men to fire, and an Indian was wounded. The chiefs insisted that their warriors not retaliate, thinking that Grattan had had his revenge. However, Grattan brazenly ordered another barrage of fire, which resulted in the death of one of the chiefs, Chief Conquering Bear. The Miniconjou Sioux, who had tried to keep their tempers under control in dealing with the pompous Grattan and his inebriated interpreter, had been pushed too far. Grattan had crossed the line, and the Indians felt that they now had justification to retaliate.

Reprisal was swift. The Indians killed Grattan, his interpreter, and a few men who were standing by the cannon. The Sixth Infantry attempted to retreat to the safe haven of Fort Laramie, but the Indians pursued them. All but one soldier were killed within a mile of the camp. Upon hearing the news from the lone soldier who had made his way back to Fort Laramie, residents and emigrants barricaded themselves in a fort, fearful of further attack.

Meanwhile, the enraged Sioux, realizing that their annuity from Uncle Sam would now most likely not be forthcoming, raided the nearby trading post. After taking what they felt was their due, they reportedly set fire to the outer buildings of Fort Laramie and then withdrew across the river.

After reporting the shooting of the cows at Fort Laramie, the Danish Mormon wagon train had pulled out of camp, not realizing the horrific consequences. Two Mormon brothers who had lingered behind caught up with the wagon train to report that thirty soldiers had been killed at Fort Laramie. The Mormon train then joined three other smaller companies for protection. It remains unclear if they fully realized the impact of reporting the cow incident.

The Grattan Massacre had severe repercussions. The tenuous peace between the emigrants and the Indians had been shattered, and the Plains Wars—a twenty-five year period of intermittent indiscriminate retaliation between the U.S. military and the Sioux and Cheyenne Indians—had begun. Travel along the Oregon Trail had become more dangerous because of Lieutenant Grattan's poor handling of an incident as trivial as the shooting of two cows.

By 1900, practically all Native Americans had been corralled on reservations. Their attempt to protect and preserve their ancestral lands by banding together with various tribes proved to be no match for the encroaching American citizens with the U.S. military behind them. The tidal wave of emigrants coming along the Oregon Trail engulfed the continent and literally took over the land.

A Trail Delicacy

•1854•

Sixteen-year-old Sarah Johnson Cannon looked down at her dusty brown bare feet as she walked alongside her family's sluggish wagon train as it plodded along over the Oregon Trail. At the pace of 2 miles per hour, it felt to Sarah that this place called Oregon might as well be on the other side of the world. Just getting to Independence Rock was taking long enough.

This Fourth of July promised to be memorable if the Cannons' wagon train could reach its destination on time. According to the guidebooks, arriving at Independence Rock by the Fourth of July meant that they were advancing on schedule, and that's exactly what they planned to do.

The very identifiable mammoth outcropping of rock was said to be impossible to miss. When Sarah noticed an isolated lump on the horizon miles down the road, she knew she had spotted it. As the caravan pulled closer to the ever-growing chunk of granite, a collective sense of excitement pulsed through the emigrants. Soon the festivities could begin.

The Sweetwater River, running alongside Independence Rock, was an ideal spot for a layover. In the distance Sarah could see that many caravans were encamped there. Buffalo and grizzly bears could be seen in the vicinity as well, yet Sarah Cannon and her brothers barely took notice of them. All eyes were fixed on the giant, lopsided rock, which the guidebook had calculated to be 193 feet tall at the north end and 167 feet tall at the south end. Sarah just stood there with her mouth gaping open as she took in its size.

People were climbing up Independence Rock to carve their names or initials on its surface, and the surrounding area was bustling with activity. Clearly the Cannons weren't the only ones who were looking forward to celebrating the Fourth of July in style. Everyone was in a festive mood. The wagons encamped along the bank of the Sweetwater River displayed either an American flag or a facsimile of one. A variety of articles were hoisted up on sticks. Handkerchiefs or clothing served as a substitute if no American flag was available.

Then there was the music. Fiddlers were fiddlin' right in the middle of the day. Some happy-go-lucky emigrants engaged in a lively square dance, and children were frolicking and splashing about in the river. Among the peals of laughter and spirited conversations could be heard the rising voices of self-pronounced orators giving patriotic speeches amid circles of interested emigrants. The entire scene resembled a town gathering.

To Sarah's surprise, as her eyes rose above the commotion and scanned Independence Rock to its pinnacle, she saw precariously perched on the summit what looked like a covered wagon and a tent. Closer examination revealed them to be so. There, atop Independence Rock for all to see, was an emigrant's wagon. Its owner was in the process of making and selling apple pies. Dried apple pies! Quite the unexpected and delectable treat this far from Sarah's home in Clinton, Iowa. It made Sarah giggle to think that two-fifths of the way into her cross-country journey, some 830 miles from civilization, there was this bakery of sorts. Surely such an undertaking took an immeasurable amount of energy to execute. Sarah certainly admired the "baker's" entrepreneurial spirit, but she marveled even more at just how this wagon had gotten to the very top. It was amazing enough that the emigrants themselves could climb up the sides of Independence Rock on foot, but hoisting a heavy wagon up so high was even harder to imagine.

To make the Fourth of July a bit more celebratory, many a cook had been saving something special to dish up. Everyone was weary of the trail diet of salt pork, hardtack bread, bacon, and beans, so the addition of a delectable apple dessert was the perfect complement to an Independence Day feast. Sarah remarked, "No doubt this was the most elevated 'pie counter' of any of that time from the Missouri River to Portland."

Carefree and happy moments, no matter how small, were not taken for granted along the trail. Sarah enjoyed the opportunity that day to talk and share experiences with other young girls her age. The hardships of traveling and living out-of-doors, the lack of provisions on the trail, and the universal homesickness were more tolerable when shared with others. For the leaders of the assembled wagon trains, stopping over at Independence Rock was a chance to compare notes and seek advice from the more experienced travelers. The festivities and the "pie wagon" made for an enjoyable and memorable day at Independence Rock in July of 1854 for Sarah and every other emigrant looking for excitement.

These early pioneers had come to settle and tame a land called Oregon by migrating westward along the Oregon Trail. Two years after arriving in southern Oregon, just before her nineteenth birthday, Sarah wed twenty-five-year-old Sam Handsaker, who had emigrated a year ahead of the Cannon family. Together they and their eight children worked hard to forge a life for themselves out of the wilderness. Perhaps every time Sarah served apple pie on subsequent Independence Days she thought of the one she had enjoyed at the "elevated pie counter" along the Oregon Trail. Of the countless tales Sarah could tell her children and grandchildren about her overland journey across the country as a young girl, perhaps the "sweetest" was the day she had stopped at Independence Rock on the Fourth of July.

Push Me, Pull Me

•1856•

Standing in the light rain on the bow of the old clipper ship, Elizabeth could see the silhouettes of two men making their way through the blanket of fog. The men were looking up from the dock below, intent on seeking out someone in the crowd of immigrants assembled on the deck. Thinking that she recognized the dark figures, Elizabeth drew up the collar of her cloak to hide her face as she hurriedly moved her children away from the railing. The last thing she wanted was another ugly scene.

When she heard her name called out, Elizabeth turned and faced her two brothers, who had come aboard the ship as it waited in the English harbor. One by one, all five of Elizabeth's children, ranging in age from five to nineteen years, came out from behind their mother. Elizabeth's brothers implored her not to take the children on what they deemed to be a perilous journey across the Atlantic Ocean, much less an overland pilgrimage in a foreign land. Elizabeth's intention of following the primitive path referred to as the Oregon Trail was, in their minds, nothing short of ludicrous for a widow with five children.

Elizabeth had resolutely rejected her brothers' offer to give her financial security if she would remain in England. To Elizabeth, security was spiritual, not financial, and all efforts to dissuade her were in vain. Considering the hardship her family was to experience on their cross-country trek, one has to wonder how many times the children revisited that scene on the ship and whether they wished their mother had taken their uncles' advice.

After nearly two turbulent months at sea crossing the Atlantic Ocean, Elizabeth and her family arrived on the East Coast of America. They continued by train to Kanesville (Council Bluffs), Iowa, which was where the Mormons gathered before beginning their journey to the promised land.

Elizabeth Simpson Haigh Bradshaw, twice widowed, was a Mormon convert. In sailing to America and traveling overland by wagon to Utah, she was following Brigham Young's "Divine Plan" for the European Mormons, members of the Church of Latter-day Saints. In Kanesville, Elizabeth and her family banded with other Saints, as they were known, and joined the Martin Handcart Company.

Aiding the vast numbers of impoverished European converts determined to cross the continent and settle in Utah proved to be an expensive enterprise for the Mormon Church. Church officials decided that providing wagons for everyone was cost prohibitive. Forced to cut costs somewhere, officials told the travel-weary believers to pile their belongings into two-wheeled handcarts instead of wagons when they arrived in Iowa.

To make matters worse, there were not enough handcarts for the number of Saints arriving. Additional carts were hastily constructed out of unseasoned oak or hickory, and Elizabeth and her company were delayed in starting out as they waited for their carts to be built. Guidebooks recommended starting out on the Oregon Trail sometime between the last week of April and the end of May. An earlier start date would not allow the grasses on the plains to be high enough to sustain the oxen on the journey. Leaving later could bring them dangerously close to encountering early winter snowstorms. It was July 15 before the Martin Handcart Company was ready to set out. The Willie Handcart Company wouldn't be prepared to leave until even later, on July 26. The decision to leave at such a late date was put to a vote, and all but an experienced cross-country traveler voted in the affirmative.

Obeying the officials of the church, Elizabeth and the others were expected to continue their journey on foot across the country. Fortunately, each handcart company was given two wagons, which carried food supplies and tents. The emigrants, however, carried everything else. They were to position themselves between the short front handles and pull the carts behind them like oxen would. Each handcart was 7 feet long from the back to the tip of the handles and had two 58-inch wheels. The box, or cargo area, itself was 3 feet wide, 4 feet long, and 8 inches deep. Into that, Elizabeth piled the personal provisions for her family of six: Adults were allotted seventeen pounds and children ten pounds each.

The Mormon Trail paralleled the Oregon Trail when it picked up the Platte River in Nebraska and stretched on through Wyoming, into Utah. In an attempt to avoid contact with the non-Mormon travelers, or gentiles, migrating on the same river path, Elizabeth and the other Mormons traveled along the north bank of the Platte River.

Camped outside in a tent night after night, the Saints braved all sorts of weather, only to trudge on the next day. Older children could take turns with the adults in dragging or pushing the family cart along in what is described as one of the worst treks westward. When the unseasoned wood shrank in the blistering sun, causing those carts' wheels to fall apart, the remaining carts were overloaded with other people's provisions. This greatly slowed the progress of the company. But, with God as their moral compass, Elizabeth, her children, and the members of the Martin Handcart Company pressed on.

To lighten their load and to hasten their progress through present-day Wyoming, the Mormons were directed to cut their lading almost in half, and therefore parted with many supplies. Not long afterward they found themselves caught in winter storms, desperately wishing they had their discarded blankets, clothing, and food. Weakened from hunger, fatigue, and the extremes of weather, the emigrants could barely muster the energy to go on.

While the north bank of the Platte River had fewer river crossings, it still had its share of dangers. These Mormon converts could not afford the established bridge tolls and were consequently forced to wade through freezing water. During one crossing, Elizabeth and her youngest child, whom she was carrying on her shoulders, were swept downstream. Both narrowly escaped drowning. The weak could not withstand the hardship of the grueling pilgrimage, and the emigrants began the first of many burials.

The first three handcart companies that set out in 1856 arrived safely, but the remaining four suffered terribly. Stunned by the early winter storms, which hit on October 19, the poorly clad travelers could not brave the 18 inches of snow and the sub-zero temperatures. Most of the 145 members of the Martin Handcart Company perished on a 60-mile stretch between Bessermen Bend, the uppermost crossing of the North Platte River, and Martin's Cove, near Devil's Gate. Freezing ground made it difficult to dig the many graves.

Relief teams sent out by Brigham Young met what was left of Elizabeth's stranded party on November 1. Nearly one month later the survivors were brought to Salt Lake City, dazed to find that they were still alive. Survivors sustained lost limbs or extremities and suffered from physical impairments for the rest of their lives. Harsh weather on the Oregon Trail had claimed many of the believers, but Elizabeth and all five of her children had somehow found the strength to persevere and were fortunate not to suffer any permanent damage.

Elizabeth Simpson Haigh Bradshaw never remarried. She called Utah, where she lived with her children, home until her death at age sixty-four. She had forsaken a life of relative wealth and comfort in her native England for one of religious servitude, humbling herself before God. Though her family and friends back home may have thought that she marched to the beat of a different drummer, Elizabeth Simpson Haigh Bradshaw was not alone. In search of religious freedom, 70,000 other Mormons made a pilgrimage to Utah. Three percent of that number journeyed between 1856 and 1860 in a total of ten handcart companies.

The following song was familiar to many whose voices joined together in faith and hope of reaching their promised land:

The Handcart Song
(sung by the Saints on the Mormon Trail)

Ye Saints who dwell on Europe's shore,
Prepare yourselves for many more,
To leave behind your native land,
For sure God's judgments are at hand.
For you must cross the raging main
Before the promised land you gain,
And with the faithful make a start,
To cross the plains with your handcart.

Chorus:
For some must push and some must pull,
As we go marching up the hill,
So merrily on the way we go
Until we reach the valley, O!

Words by John Daniel Thompson McAllister (circa 1850)

Girl Overboard

•1859•

The blood-curdling scream reverberated up and down the length of the wagon train for some distance, rising above the plodding of the oxen's feet, the creaking of the wagons, and the general hum of conversations. All those who heard the cry immediately felt the hair rise on the backs of their necks and a pit form in their stomachs. Something terrible had happened.

Above the whirring of the whips cracking in the air, the strong voices of the men commanded the oxen to stop. As the wagons ground to a halt, they caused the dust to rise to an impenetrable cloud blocking the vision of man and beast. Above the din rose anguished cries from one of the wagons.

Ira and Elizabeth True and their four children from Owatonna, Minnesota, were traveling the Oregon Trail to the West Coast. Their eight-wagon caravan was part of the great throng of emigrants migrating west in 1859. Ira True had been riding up ahead of the train with the captain, seeking out a good noonday rest stop, when the two men heard a faint panicked cry and the halting of the wagons. It was clear that the safety of someone in the group was in question. With hearts pounding, they raced back to the wagon train to discern what had happened. There, lying alongside the trail, Ira found his youngest daughter injured and in shock in her mother's arms and his eldest son dust-covered and dazed. Members of the train who had come to help encircled them all.

It had all happened so quickly. Sixteen-year-old Charley True was in charge of driving the wagon for his family that day. The path along the southern bank of the Platte River was somewhat rough, but relatively level, and Charley was an experienced and confident driver who was handling the bumpy road well. When Charley heard his mother's terrified shout, he loosened his grip on the reins and turned his head in her direction. It was as if everything were happening in slow motion. There on the ground below Charley was his four-year-old sister, Carro, who had somehow fallen from the wagon. The front wheel of their 3,000-pound wagon had just rolled over her tiny body.

Charley snapped into action. He had but seconds to act. If Carro's dress was caught in the wagon, it could turn her writhing and helpless form and put her small, bonneted head in the direct path of the rear wagon wheel. Charley flew off the driver's seat and flung his body in the direction of his sister's, somewhere in the dust cloud below. Wrapping his arms around whatever part of her that he could grab, he hugged her to himself and together they rolled over and over away from the wagon.

Once they stopped tumbling and ended up beyond the cloud of dust, Charley had a chance to actually see Carro. The little girl lay there crumpled in her torn and ragged dress. By then their mother had scrambled out of the wagon, after bringing it to a stop, and crawled to where her two children lay prostrate on the ground. Her eyes were wide with fear. Not knowing the extent of their injuries, she quickly checked their heads and limbs, examining and assessing as only a mother can do. Charley's quick thinking and desperate action had saved Carro's life, though her leg had been broken by the weight of the wagon.

As the onlookers stared down at the injured girl, the same thoughts went through their heads. Wagon-wheel accidents claimed the youngest of victims along the Trail. Children got so used to clambering in and out of their wagons that they lost respect for the danger the vehicles presented. The habit of jumping from the tongue of a wagon before it was brought to a halt was dangerous. A slip into the turning spokes of the wheel could quickly bring someone down, particularly the girls with their long skirts, but everyone did it. Surely Mrs. True had implored the children countless times not to lean out of the wagon. Perhaps she had turned her head for an instant when, for whatever reason, little Carro had toppled over and under and the heavily laden wagon could not be stopped in time.

Accidents were a risk inherent in overland travel. The outcome sometimes depended on where the nearest doctor was. Carro's fall had occurred just north of Fort Kearney, a few hundred miles from where the family had "jumped off" at Omaha, Nebraska. The Trues' worst fears had been realized—there was no doctor in sight.

Carro's leg had been broken below the knee. There were no volunteers who felt capable of setting the bone. This responsibility fell upon Mr. True, who was acutely aware that if set correctly, the limb would heal properly and allow Carro to walk again, but that a poor job would leave her crippled for life.

No wood could be found along this section of the treeless Platte River, so dry willow reeds were collected to make a splint for Carro's leg. Ira True whittled them down to the correct size, dreading what he had to do next for his daughter. Poor, terrified Carro screamed at the top of her lungs in pain as her father set the broken limb. The sight of this brought her mother to the point of hysteria. Some members of the train eventually had to remove Mrs. True and her other children from the scene so that her husband could complete the agonizing task. Being spared from seeing the torture that Carro was undergoing did little to appease the anxious Mrs. True, however. After being reunited with her daughter, the distraught mother did all that she could to calm Carro, who desperately needed to rest after her ordeal.

Speed was of the essence along the Oregon Trail, though, as the emigrants had to reach their destination before the onset of the winter snows. No matter what happened along the Trail—an accident, a birth, or a death—there was no time to lay over. Delaying the trip so that Carro's break could mend was just not possible, yet the jarring action from the rough road would certainly prevent the injury from healing properly.

Fellow traveler Harry Cavill solved the dilemma. He gave his coveted spring wagon seat to the tiny victim. Others made a makeshift bed of pillows upon the seat, which was attached to the inside of the Trues' wagon. Little Carro rested there, strapped firmly to the spring bed, which cushioned her from the jostling motion along the bumpy road.

Immobilized for weeks along the hot and dusty Trail, Carro had little to do but lie there and recover. When her siblings had done everything they could to entertain her, Carro played with her doll. She also basked in "Poor Little Prinnie's" unswerving attention. The family's pet dog, one-year-old Prince, also needed to heal from injury—his paws were bleeding from the many hours of walking on hot sand. He lay there faithfully, beneath the spring bed, guarding his charge. The two injured travelers passed the days and hours together in the sanctuary of their covered wagon.

After what must have seemed like an eternity to Carro, her splints were taken off. To the great joy of everyone in the caravan, Carro's broken leg had healed completely. The Trues continued along the Oregon Trail and survived the many trials and tribulations that were part of overland travel. They escaped a prairie fire, a buffalo stampede, an unfriendly Indian encounter, and a nearly unbearable desert crossing. Being greatly inconvenienced by the loss of basic necessities, they were fatigued to the point of failing and sadly had to part with many of their prized belongings to lighten their load. What was left of their team, an oddly matched cow and ox duo, carried them over the last miles of the Trail.

Charley True's quick thinking during his sister's accident had saved the girl from incurring more serious damage, or even death. Totally unimpaired by her Trail injury, the lively little Carro went on to become an acclaimed actress in San Francisco.

Wish Upon a Falling Star

•1860•

It was a chaotic scene in the crowded, bustling jumping-off town of Independence, Missouri. The southeast corner of the square, which was known as the official start of the Oregon Trail, was the place to be. That's where newcomers came to mingle with and get advice from those emigrants who were ready to pull out. The new arrivals relied on word-of-mouth to find the best deals in town, from supplies and provisions to food and lodging.

Each spring the small jumping-off towns along the Missouri River were bursting at the seams. Thousands of westbound emigrants descended on the outfitting towns and camped for days or weeks while preparing for the overland journey. Businesses seemed to pop up almost overnight to serve the multitudes of emigrants pouring into Independence, and generally the hotels were squalid. From conversations heard in the town square, it was clear that some emigrant women were livid about the conditions of the sleeping apartment their families had to share with other travelers. Apparently reeling from the previous night's stay in one of the town's hotels, a hysterical young mother was in the process of enumerating all that was distressing her. Forget the raucous carrying-on coming from the rowdy saloon below them until all hours of the night. Never mind the seedy lowlifes that had stayed in the room next to them. What provoked this woman was that her family had to stay in the despicable, unhygienic establishment that the owner had the audacity to call a "hotel."

The disgusting bedbugs, the rancid water in the wash-basin, and the rank food with its putrid odor, had nearly made them all ill. It didn't seem to help when the woman's husband, in a pathetic attempt to calm his tearful wife, had reminded her that soon they would be roughing it on the Oregon Trail—where conditions might be even worse.

Amid the commotion in the square, a sympathetic emigrant woman who had heard the young mother complaining took a moment to commiserate with her. Yes, the conditions in most of the local establishments were revolting. But she could recommend a hotel in town that was unlike all the others.

Every prospective traveler knew that life on the Oregon Trail would provide many challenging experiences. It would be months before any of the westbound travelers would see any semblance of civilization. But after traveling to reach frontier towns, many emigrants—particularly the women—were hoping to spend one last night in a decent hotel before heading out.

Steamboats carrying covered wagons left daily from St. Louis, Missouri. Heading west, they traveled upstream for some 350 miles and unloaded at one of several frontier towns along the Missouri River. Perhaps the most exciting place to live during the wagon-train era was the town of Independence, on the south side of the Missouri River. Independence was perfectly situated for "jumping off" onto the Trail. This outfitting center served many pioneers heading west on the Oregon Trail. There was profit to be made in the rough-and-rowdy frontier town, and a woman named Emily Fisher was set up to take advantage of it.

Emily Fisher had worked as a slave for Adam Fisher for many years. Mr. Fisher had a large farm located east of Independence on Jones Road. Emily Fisher and her husband, Rowan, their sons, Shelby and Rowan Jr., and their daughter, Sarah, worked as slaves on the Fisher farm. While the men worked in the gristmill, Emily worked as Mr. Fisher's housekeeper.

Emily Fisher had no idea that the training she received while working as a housekeeper in her master's house would prepare her for her duties as a hotelier. Shortly before his death in 1860, Adam Fisher, her master and her father, decided to free Emily—sometime in the late 1850s. The woman was then in her early forties. Knowing full well that by simply freeing Emily he would be doing her no favor, Adam Fisher sought to find a means for Emily to support herself.

Since Emily had become a hard-working woman who had excellent housekeeping skills, Adam Fisher had decided to set her up in the business of running a hotel. Emily was grateful to have a chance at a better life.

Many westbound travelers found their way to the doors of Emily fisher's hotel—including the distraught young woman on the square. This was one hotel that had earned the respect of the shopkeepers and businesses in town, along with the visitors who stopped over.

Fisher's establishment was a welcome contrast to the unsanitary conditions in many parts of the transient and congested town. Emily Fisher ran her hotel as she saw fit, providing a hygienic rest stop, a last taste of comfort for emigrants. She had heard stories of how harsh life on the Trail was, and in her opinion, the Oregon-bound travelers would be roughing it soon enough, sleeping out-of-doors in makeshift tents, braving the elements, and consuming the same monotonous diet for months on end. The last thing the emigrants wanted to do was waste their savings on disgusting overnight accommodations in Independence, only to wish later that they had the money for river crossings or for supplies from the trading posts. Under Fisher's roof, the emigrants could have one last night to enjoy the basic comforts of home—a clean bed and a good meal. Known for her strong character, and with a firm belief in God's provision,

Emily Fisher worked tirelessly to consistently provide sanitary lodgings.

Sometimes after things had settled down for the evening, Fisher would step outdoors and look up at the sky. It was hard to believe that these were the same stars she had gazed upon as a child, back on her master's farm. Each night Fisher had fixed her eyes upon the brightest star and made a wish. But she had never dared to dream so big as to think that one day she would be able to earn a living rather than be a slave.

Emily Fisher was determined to make a difference in other people's opinions of whether a freed slave could succeed in a white society. She did not intend to let anything stop her from making a go of her hotel, and her belief in the reward of hard work carried Fisher through. Word spread of the high standards in her establishment, and her hotel flourished. This allowed Fisher and her family to raise their station in life. Fisher proudly saw her children freed from bondage, educated, and established in respectable careers. Her hotel was a successful venture until the time of the Civil War, when business declined. Reportedly the industrious Emily Fisher found another way to make a living; she developed a healing salve and traveled throughout the area selling the ointment from a wooden bucket.

Fisher lived out her life in Independence, enjoying her many grandchildren. She died at the age of ninety and was buried in the Woodlawn Cemetery in an unmarked grave. Almost one hundred years later, a monument was erected in her memory in the Fisher family plot in the cemetery, thanks to the Community of Concerned Citizens in Independence, Missouri. The town of Independence has chosen to honor her as well, inscribing her name on a plaque near the Pioneer Woman statue at the National Frontier Trails Center in Independence.

It is said that Emily's homemaking skills live on in her descendants. Her great-granddaughter, Vietta Garr, achieved similar fame. She had been Harry S. Truman's cook in

Independence, Missouri, and the Trumans were very fond of her. When President Truman was in Washington, D.C., he brought Vietta Garr with him to instruct the White House kitchen staff how to cook the "Missouri way." Like her great-grandmother before her, Vietta brought the comforts of home to a transcontinental traveler.

A Trip to the Moon, Anyone?

• 1864 •

Mountain ranges, majestic natural landmarks, buffalo herds, prairie dogs, and even warring Indians were some of the sights Julius Caesar Merrill may have expected to see on his trip out West, but nothing could have prepared him for what he stood looking at now. Far from his home in Milwaukee, Wisconsin, on that 28th day of April, 1864, Merrill and his caravan were crossing through south-central Idaho on Goodale's Cutoff.

Very abruptly they had entered into a foreign land. Gone were the sands of the unchanging desertlike scenery. There before them was an uninhabitable, treeless area of volcanic debris. The debris stretched for miles, sprinkled in a field of rock clefts and crags. This barren land was filled with spattered volcanic formations ranging from black cinder cones resembling mini-volcanoes to dry, hardened lava tubes and irregular lava flows. The fingers of the solidified lava flows felt their way across the desert terrain, spreading out in a haphazard pattern of mounds and cones.

At first the settlers were dumbstruck. Then everyone began to talk at once. The bewildered emigrants dropped to the desert floor to touch the sharp-edged, porous lava rocks and then scurried about to explore their new surroundings. The captain of their wagon train surveyed the area on horseback.

This surreal landscape, coarse and charred as it was, possessed a beauty of its own.

The awesome force of the earth had revealed itself, and though it was awe-inspiring, Julius Merrill knew what it meant. This forbidding obstacle that now stood in their way presented yet another new challenge that was certain to slow the caravan's progress.

The settlers' time through this strange land was a study in contrasts. At night when the sun set, the temperatures dropped. The emigrants set up their evening camp on the outskirts of the lava flows and tried to keep warm. The moonlight on the striking sterile landscape created an eerie-yet-captivating aura, with shadows that danced on the strange, irregular shapes. The emigrants' heads were filled with wild imaginings.

The warmth of the morning light woke the travelers with a hint of what was to come. The intense summer sun during the day reached 90 degrees in July, and the surface temperature of the hard lava was 150 to 175 degrees Fahrenheit, which made it impossible to walk barefoot. The razor-sharp lava rocks tore through shoes and ripped the oxen's hooves to shreds. The wagon wheels, already tenuously held inside their iron rims due to shrinkage in the blistering heat of the sun, certainly could not stand the jarring motion of traveling over these hardened, irregular mounds. The emigrants' only choice was to skirt the edge of the lava flows, causing the wagon train to take a most circuitous route. They turned north to circumvent the massive volcanic topography, but sometimes there was no choice but to traverse the solid streamlike fissures and remove the jagged lava rocks that littered the landscape as the caravan forged on.

Each new day in this bizarre landscape was full of curious wonders and challenges. Then the lavalike terrain ended as abruptly as it had begun. The starkness of the black, hardened eruptions gave way to the Little Wood River Valley at Fish Creek. The next section of the Trail crossed a mountain range and went down into a valley of lush, green grass, through which Silver Creek meandered. The contrast of color and terrain was remarkable. From then on, the remainder of Goodale's Cutoff was easier to travel, but none of the emigrants would soon forget what they had just been through on those 30 waterless miles. Those who had opted to stay on the main route of the Oregon Trail farther south along the Snake River never knew of the lava landscape. The volcanic formations did not reach that far south.

Merrill wrote in his diary, "It was a desolate, dismal scenery. Up or down the valley as far as the eye could reach or across the mountains and into the dim distance the same unvarying mass of black rock. Not a shrub, bird, nor insect seemed to live near it. Great must have been the relief of the volcano, powerful the emetic, that poured such a mass of black vomit."

Merrill's wagon train was not the first to use this route. It had been forged ten years earlier and then rediscovered by celebrated mountaineer and guide Tim Goodale. Goodale had led one of the largest emigrant trains ever over this cutoff two years earlier in an attempt to avoid contact with unfriendly Indians. Those settlers who continued to use it named the bizarre cutoff after him.

As he crossed the lava beds, Merrill saw no signs of life, and he thought nothing could exist on this barren land. But nature, in its infinite ability to adapt, does sustain life here in the milder fall and spring seasons. The land is home to 300 plant species, 148 types of birds, 47 species of mammals, 2,000 species of insects, 8 types of reptiles, and 1 amphibian, the western toad.

With its 618 square miles, this odd volcanic area is the largest lava field in the lower contiguous United States. It is perhaps one of the best places to study the effects of volcanoes. In the early 1900s this particular section of Goodale's Cutoff was named "Craters of the Moon" for its lunaresque landscape. In 1969 Apollo astronauts even came to the area to train for their missions—an occurrence Merrill and his companions could never have imagined back in 1864.

Clouded Vision

•1865•

When the moon was completely hidden by clouds high above the flat expanse of open prairie, it was as black as pitch. Dancing on the voice of the night wind were the eerie cries of the coyotes. The reluctant sentry imagined he could even hear the "war whoops" of the Indians across the plains. Even the smallest of noises seemed to resonate in the air, setting the reluctant guard's nerves on edge. The emigrant's shift for sentry duty was well under way, and he loathed this responsibility.

Hands trembling, he tapped his index finger nervously against the smooth metal trigger of his black-barreled rifle while his thumb hovered over the serrated flintlock. The rise and fall of his own heavy breathing and the pounding of his pulsating heart had reached a crescendo in his head, which felt ready to explode. The guard knew he had heard something. If only the half moon would stop hiding behind the clouds, he could see better. No, maybe it was his imagination after all. It was nothing. He had just let the strangeness of the Trail affect his thinking. The young man knew he'd better calm down and keep a level head if he planned to keep that head attached to his shoulders on the long trek westward over the Oregon Trail.

As the young man gulped down the last of his coffee before heading out to his post in the cool night air, he again heard a sound. He dropped his tin cup on the ground, which broke the stillness of the night. The creaking of a covered wagon made him snap his head around to track the noise. It could have been an emigrant in the wagon train simply turning over in his or her sleep, or it might be an intruder. As the guard cocked his gun and looked around, peering into the darkness, a shiver ran up and down his spine.

Just as the young man was about to dismiss the sounds as part of the inevitable nightly noises, some cattle shifted and moaned. Perhaps they had detected an Indian sneaking into camp. No one could afford to lose any more horses, and the guard planned on making sure none were lost on his watch. He counted the seconds until the ominous clouds blew across the starless sky, allowing the faint moonlight to filter down. Alternately, patches of prairie were dimly illuminated and he squinted his eyes to see.

The young emigrant guard nearly jumped out of his skin when he detected a definite movement of something not that far off. Noiselessly throwing himself onto the ground of the treeless plain, he tried desperately to steady his rifle on his arm, which rested on the uneven earth.

Straining his eyes, he could make out a figure in the grass moving toward him. It looked like an Indian wrapped up in a blanket, stealthily making his way into camp in the middle of the night. Closer and closer the Indian came. Yes, the guard had him in view now. The Indian probably had a gun concealed under his blanket, as well as a tomahawk. Probably had a scalp belt dangling from his waist in proud display of his "trophies." Well, this was one less Indian that was going to be around to steal their horses. This was one less Indian who'd ever give them trouble. He'd shoot 'im dead and leave his rotten, stinkin' body for his entire tribe to see. He'd teach the whole lot of barbarians a lesson they'd not soon forget.

Though the guard's anger and disgust for the savage was mounting with every step closer the red man took, it did nothing to calm his nerves. When the Indian's blanket began to slip off his bent shoulders, it revealed an outline of the butt of a rifle. The young guard's eyes widened as fear and terror gripped him. He closed his eyes and pulled the trigger of his own weapon. The Indian fell forward and slumped to the ground, apparently dead.

The biggest threat that this particular wagon train and others suffered from the Indians along the Oregon Trail was that of thievery. Ignorant of the Indian custom of offering tokens of appreciation for traveling through foreign land, many emigrants offered no tribute at all. The Indians, fully expecting some offer of a favor, approached the wagon trains, wanting to collect their due. The emigrants interpreted this as begging and began to resent the forced gift-giving.

The attitude of the overlanders toward the Native Americans ranged from superiority and disgust to intrigue and friendship. Broken treaties and confinement on reservations were generally thought to be the Indians' lot in life. The white man's high-wheeled wagons with their billowing tops inched across the continent, boldly claiming more and more Indian land. Over the years relations between the two groups worsened.

The single greatest cause for the strained relations was indiscriminate retaliation. This was the cause of the young guard's near-frenzy this particular evening. Sometimes unsuspecting individuals and groups paid for deeds they hadn't committed when attacks were launched by either party. It is not known what stories this emigrant-turned-sentry-guard had heard. Exaggerated accounts of molestations, torture, and killings traveled like wildfire among the wagon trains. The rare but severe atrocities committed by both sides gave way to extremes of prejudice and hatred of people unlike themselves.

It was no wonder, then, that the young emigrant guard felt justified in pulling the trigger on that cold, moonless night on the lonely prairie in 1865. His job was to protect the people in his wagon train and their livestock. So as the guard recoiled from the kick of his gun, the camp was awakened to a flurry of excitement and fear. Terror quickly spread throughout the startled caravan. As rifles and guns were cocked and shouts of "Who goes there?" rang out, the captain of the one-hundred-wagon caravan, William Wesley White, ran toward the sentry post.

The young guard, back on his feet, made his way toward the fallen, blanketed figure, shouting, "That Indian will never steal any more stock!" As he yanked the blanket off the savage to make sure he was dead, a sliver of moonlight fell upon the face of his own father. The beloved Baptist minister, the preacher who had endeared himself to all in the wagon train, had wrapped himself up in a blanket before taking his post as guard on that chilly night.

Realizing that he had shot and killed his own father, the young man nearly lost his mind. The ugly result that fear and prejudice can bring forth had become painfully clear to everyone in the train. The stunned son was sickened with remorse. His father had meant so much to so many.

Historian Fred Lockley interviewed Mrs. W. C. Kantner for her recollections about crossing the plains as a child. Mrs. Kantner was a girl of nine years when she left Linn County, Missouri, for Oregon in 1865. Her brother, William Wesley White, was captain of the wagon train. This story is her most vivid memory of their journey. Though she could no longer remember the name of the Baptist minister or his son, she did recall that he was buried under the path of the Oregon Trail. To obscure the grave and prevent the Indians from digging it up, they scattered the ashes from their campfire over the grave site and rolled their caravan over it.

Capturing History in the Making

•1886•

After trying one get-rich-quick scheme after another, Solomon Butcher finally thought he had a sure thing. Why not capture history as it happened in Custer County, Nebraska, by photographing pioneers who traveled the Oregon Trail? The year was 1886 and some residents of Custer County laughed outright at Butcher for trying to capture the history of an area that didn't even have a history yet.

Butcher and his family, who were originally from West Virginia, had been in Nebraska for eight years. Butcher knew all too well what it took to carve out a life for oneself on the plains. Restless by nature, he found that settling down to the rigorous life of a homesteader was not for him. Therefore, at age thirty he embarked on a new career as a frontier photographer.

Americans were spreading across the country, and for Butcher, that spelled opportunity. As pioneers began to feel fenced in when neighbors arrived, they continually pushed further west to settle new land. Thus, the frontier border moved west accordingly. The Great Plains of the interior of the continent was generally perceived as an undesirable wasteland. Emigrants sometimes referred to it as the "Great American Desert" because the lack of trees and tough prairie sod made it seem like a desert. Until the 1860s this region had been merely a corridor through which the pioneers traveled to their West Coast destinations, but that was beginning to change.

Disregarding the fact that the land actually belonged to the native Indians, the U.S. government had begun offering free, fertile farmland by opening up new territories for settlement by the 1850s. Not only were emigrants stopping midway along the Oregon Trail to farm this land; the Transcontinental Railroad was also bringing record numbers of people right to Butcher's doorstep in the state of Nebraska. There was money to be made.

The westward expansion of America coincided with the growth and popularity of photography, the new invention that made it possible to capture live images on paper. The first prototype images had been made in 1839, and by the 1850s photography had captured the interest of the general population. In fact, photography may have played some role in the settlement of the West. For the first time people could see exactly what a particular far-away landscape looked like, rather than having to rely on an artist's rendering, and those pictures spurred their interest.

Butcher had an idea to use photography somewhat differently. To keep in touch, pioneers on the plains wrote letters to family and friends back home. Perhaps they might also want to send photographs of themselves, which would better enable them to share a part of their lives with loved ones back east. If people were willing to pay to have their photographs taken precisely for this purpose, they could send those they'd left behind a tangible, visual reminder of themselves. The pictures might help ease the pain of their separation.

Butcher found that it was difficult to convince people of a new idea, especially one that would cost them some of their precious spare money. Therefore, instead of just selling individual portraits, Butcher took subscriptions for a book that he intended to publish. The book would be a compilation of photographs of the settlers in the county, a record of the early days that would allow future generations to have a pictorial account of their ancestors. Some settlers were intrigued, some were skeptical, and some thought Butcher was outright crazy.

Butcher persevered, however, and in the period of a few weeks he managed to sign up enough families for his book—around seventy-five—and he believed he just might see his idea come to fruition. After convincing his father that he had potential customers, he obtained some financial aid to set himself up in business. With camera equipment and wagon in hand, he set out.

The early picture-taking process was quite involved. The cameras were large and cumbersome and the sticky glass-plate negatives were heavy and fragile. But Butcher was doing what he loved. He traveled the countryside selling portraits and promoting his picture-book sales on the side.

Butcher probably had not anticipated that his job description would include hauling heavy furniture from the settlers' homes outside, but haul he did. It was customary for the pioneers to pose for pictures with items brought from their earthen sod homes, or "soddies." These prairie homes were built with the only available material, chunks of sod cut from the soil, and they weren't much to look at. Out came tables and chairs set up with the only valuables the pioneers owned, such as candlesticks, clocks, or fine china pieces. Out came heavy organs that had survived the trip on the Oregon Trail and were surely going to make it into the photograph as well. Maybe the settlers wanted to display these treasured items from back East because these things represented wealth, or perhaps it was simply that the pioneers wanted their families and friends back home to know that they enjoyed some semblance of a civilized life out on the plains.

David Hilton and his family had their photograph taken outside on their ranch in Nebraska, far from their soddie home. Mrs. Hilton was not about to have her relatives see the dirt home in which they were living. So the family gathered in front of their only prized possession, a beautiful pump organ. To the more civilized folk back home it may have seemed peculiar to see a family standing by their pump organ in the middle of a gigantic expanse of land, but to the homesteaders it may have seemed the only reasonable thing to do.

The settlers wanted everything in the photo to look just right. For most people, posing for a photograph was a life event; this would be the only time they would ever have their picture taken. Being a special, if not solemn, occasion, it called for serious expressions. Typically, the larger the family and the younger the children, the more time and energy Butcher had to expend in rounding them all up. If that proved to be too difficult, he sometimes would be instructed just to take the picture with as many family members as were there. Often just as he was about to shoot, his subjects would rearrange themselves, a stray cow would wander through, or a mother would recheck her children for dirty faces, uncombed hair, or other imperfections. While the picture-taking process could be an exercise in frustration, it wasn't worth it to upset the customer. Besides wanting to make a profit, Butcher realized that this was real life, and he felt glad to be able to capture the moment.

Butcher used what he considered to be "creative retouching" in his photographs if something didn't look right. Rather than traveling back over long distances for a time-consuming reshoot, Butcher would crudely draw in birds, trees, or whatever was needed to cover the area in question. He then had to convince the customer: "Sure enough there was a big bird on the roof, don't you remember? What do you mean it doesn't look like a bird?" He apparently thought a good sales job took less energy than retaking the photograph, and more often than not he would convince the customers to buy the photograph, even if they did shake their heads in disbelief.

While Butcher tried to make a living by capturing a photographic history of the area, he loved the stories behind the pictures even more. He saw the value in recording the stories behind these everyday people, for it seemed to add significance to their otherwise nondescript lives. He therefore documented his photographs with anecdotal information in case viewers from future generations would be genuinely interested.

The unspoken story behind the photograph of Sylvester Rawding and his family in front of their soddie home near Sargent, Nebraska, would have been lost had Butcher not recorded it. Rawding, a Union soldier during the Civil War, was twice wounded in battle. His family photograph reveals a permanent reminder of an injury Rawding received from an encounter near Mobile, Alabama. On his forehead is the visible lump from a half-inch lead musket ball that was embedded and never removed. This disfigurement was a badge of honor the brave soldier wore proudly. About a decade after the picture was taken, Rawding was forced to move to a home for old soldiers. It is said that a stepson swindled him out of his ranch, so Rawding was not able to live out his days in the soddie home he had carved out of the earth. Knowing this information makes the photograph even more special.

Butcher convinced three men who had claims next to each other, near Westerville in Custer County, Nebraska, to have their picture taken. Jerry Shores, Moses Speese, and Henry Webb insisted on being in the same picture. Butcher learned that the three men were brothers who had come west to create a good life for themselves and their families. Their last names were different because as slaves they had each taken the name of their former owner. Butcher felt that this information made the picture more interesting.

For almost forty years Butcher captured life on the Great Plains. He took more than 5,000 pictures in Nebraska, Kansas, and Colorado. The bulk of his work was from Custer County, Nebraska, where Butcher traveled tirelessly, accepting donations or trading photographs for meals and shelter.

It is said that when he died in 1927, Butcher considered himself to have been a failure, yet his life's work captured for all time the homesteading of America. His photographs and biographies of everyday people who "de-railed" from the Oregon Trail and made a life on the Great Plains offer a significant personal perspective. If Solomon Butcher had been gifted with the foresight to realize the legacy he was leaving behind, he might have measured his life differently.

Stuck in a Rut

• 1906 •

The first time Ezra Meeker traveled over the Oregon Trail was in a prairie schooner when he was twenty-one years old. Covering just 2 miles per hour, he thought the journey across the country was a once-in-a-lifetime experience. He was mistaken. The last time he traveled across the Oregon Trail was when he was ninety-four years old, flying over it in an airplane that covered 100 miles per hour. With many overland trips in between, it was clear that Ezra Meeker had a passion for the Oregon Trail.

It is estimated that 500,000 emigrants traveled on the Oregon Trail in the settling of the West from the 1840s through the 1860s. The pioneers who had survived the strenuous trek westward along the Oregon Trail were part of a story of incredible fortitude, ingenuity, heartbreak, and heroism. Ezra Meeker was not about to let this remarkable chapter in American history be forgotten, no more than he was ready to let the old ruts of the Oregon Trail be obliterated. And that was what led to his continual—some say obsessive—crisscrossing of the Trail.

Ezra Meeker's first overland journey across the Oregon Trail was similar to many other emigrants' experiences. Back in 1851 a young Ezra decided that he would marry his childhood sweetheart, Eliza Jane Sumner, a neighboring farm girl in Indianapolis, Indiana. Ezra's less-than-romantic proposal was right to the point: "I'm going to be a farmer when I get married." Some months later came Eliza Jane's answer, "Yes, I want to be a farmer, too, but I want to be a farmer on our own land." Ezra realized that he had found his soul mate, and that sealed the engagement.

With his new bride, Ezra decided to "go to Iowa, get some land, and grow up with the country." A particularly harsh winter that year, along with the difficulty in amassing funds to purchase their own Iowa farm, made the couple revise their plans. It wasn't long before Ezra and Eliza Jane began to feel the pull of "Oregon Fever" and joined the ranks of emigrants traveling westward. Little did Ezra know then that this would be only the first of his many journeys over the Oregon Trail.

With their seven-week-old son, Marion, and their one wagon, they left Indiana in the spring of 1852, looking to join a wagon train en route. With a record number of 70,000 emigrants heading west that year, they had no trouble finding amiable partners and traveling companions.

The Meekers' overland trip from the Missouri River to Portland, Oregon, took five months. Blessed with "such a life partner as the little wife," Ezra thoroughly enjoyed meeting the challenges of trail life and espoused the view that " . . . it is the small things that make up the happiness of life." Life on the Trail, though, did take its toll on both of them. Ezra, who was twenty pounds lighter than his wife, had to carry an ill Eliza Jane in his arms up the bank of the Willamette River at the end of the route. After restoring their health, Ezra and Eliza Jane set out to make a life for their family, undaunted by the fact that they had arrived with just $2.75 to their name.

Upon arriving in Oregon in October of 1852, Ezra Meeker moved his family four times before finally settling 9 miles southeast of present-day Tacoma, Washington. In 1877 they platted the town of Puyallup *(Pew-al-up),* which Ezra had named in honor of the local Indians. (He later regretted choosing a name no one could pronounce.) The Meekers attained their goal of becoming farmers. Ezra was also a merchant, a miner, a longshoreman, and a civic leader. He went on to become an entrepreneur, an author, and a historian. Ezra Meeker made millions of dollars in some of his ventures, and he also lost fortunes, only to be left rich in experience. He used his money for the betterment of society. He did everything in his power to preserve America's heritage along the historic Oregon Trail, which had become his passion later in life.

Meeker thought that he could raise awareness of the significance of the Oregon Trail through attention-drawing publicity stunts. Therefore, in 1906 the seventy-six-year-old Meeker retraced the steps that he had taken some fifty years earlier as a young pioneer on the Oregon Trail, albeit in a reverse route. Setting out from his home in Puyallup, Washington, in an oxen-drawn prairie schooner, he felt like a young man again. Meeker's destination was Washington, D.C., where he planned to meet with President Theodore Roosevelt.

Many of his contemporaries thought Meeker's idea to travel the Oregon Trail in an oxen-drawn prairie schooner in 1906 was outlandish, but there was no stopping him. Together with his dog, Jim, and driver, William Marden, and his oxen, Dave and Dandy, he began a journey that was to last more than eleven months. His goal was to draw as much attention to himself as he could. He made numerous stops, lecturing wherever he could get an audience—schools, clubs, and historical societies—and drumming up interest in preserving the Oregon Trail and establishing its rightful place in history.

Wherever he went, Meeker's presence raised attention and publicity. The sight of an ox team and covered wagon traveling the Oregon Trail—along with the seventy-six-year-old's own enthusiasm and zeal for his cause—drew photographers and reporters. Generally, Meeker was enthusiastically received. If an unfavorable account of the rather disheveled-looking overland traveler was reprinted back home in the newspaper, though, the town took it as a personal affront and was up in arms.

Meeker visited his hometown of Indianapolis, Indiana, which he had left fifty-four years earlier, and spoke and wrote about the Oregon Trail. He then left for the White House, where he was well received by President Roosevelt. By this time Meeker was not only nationally renowned, he had succeeded in bringing to the attention of the American public the importance of the Trail's history. He asked for funding for the Oregon Trail preservation project. President Roosevelt promised to give the idea serious consideration.

Meeker next traveled the Oregon Trail back to his home in Washington state, this time by train. He continued his efforts to educate the public about preserving the Oregon Trail. His dedication to his country's heritage compelled him to write effusively about it, and an author was born.

Ezra Meeker was making plans for his next ox-team trip across the country when his beloved wife, Eliza Jane, died on October 15, 1909. Eliza Jane had supported Ezra in all his business ventures, raised their four children, and was instrumental in settling Puyallup. While accompanying Ezra on a business trip to England, she met Queen Victoria, which influenced her taste. After living in log cabins for thirty-eight years, the Meekers built a Victorian mansion. They lived in their grand home for twenty years and it was from there that Eliza Jane read newspaper accounts about Ezra's historic first crossing of the Oregon Trail in his covered wagon.

Ezra had convinced Americans of the significance of the Trail, but he now needed to spur them to action. He wanted townspeople to raise money to erect markers along the Oregon Trail as it passed through their community. In 1910, at age eighty, he began a trip to identify historic spots along the Oregon Trail and properly mark them. The two-year-long trip entailed much research and many interviews. Meeker collaborated on several books about the Trail and took his message to schools. He said, "I longed to go back over the old Oregon Trail and mark it for all time for the children of the pioneers who blazed it, and for the world." Meeker continued to be welcomed wherever he went, making headlines, being greeted by city officials, and receiving keys to the city. He urged the interested throngs of people to erect monuments along the Trail's path.

Meeker was determined to get the word out to even more Americans. In 1916, in his eighty-fifth year, he traveled the Oregon Trail in a twelve-cylinder Pathfinder automobile to Washington, D.C. He addressed the U.S. Senate in an effort to establish the Oregon Trail as a military highway. Yet with all his accomplishments, Meeker still was not sure that the public was doing enough. He wanted every identifiable section of the Oregon Trail to be recognized with markers. He helped people raise funds to put up plaques and erect monuments along the sections of the Trail that passed through, or near, their towns.

At age ninety-four, Meeker came up with what he thought was a brilliant attention-drawing idea—he'd fly across the Oregon Trail in an airplane. And indeed he did travel above the Trail in an open-cockpit plane to Dayton, Ohio, with a U.S. Army pilot, Lieutenant Oakley G. Kelley. This well-publicized trip took four hours; his first overland trip had taken five months.

Meeker then left Dayton to meet with President Calvin Coolidge at the White House. Ezra Meeker had founded the Oregon Trail Memorial Association, and he persuaded Congress to pass the bill authorizing the coinage of six million fifty-cent Oregon Trail Memorial silver coins.

In yet another attempt to arouse public interest, Meeker appeared in a Wild West show when he was ninety-five years old to demonstrate how an ox team had been driven in the wagon train era. Claiming to be "the world's oldest broadcaster," he spoke on the radio about the importance of marking and preserving the Oregon Trail, thrilled that his message could reach so many.

Shortly before his ninety-eighth birthday in 1928, Meeker was preparing for yet another publicity stunt. Henry Ford had donated an automobile fitted out to look like a prairie schooner, called the "Oxmobile," for Ezra to drive on his next trip over the Oregon Trail. It was to be quite the publicity stunt. Sadly, Meeker became ill shortly before this trip and had to cancel his plans. A train brought the sorely disappointed Meeker back to Puyallup, where he died a few months later.

Ezra Meeker truly exemplified the spirit and determination of America's early pioneers. He helped to commemorate the Oregon Trail for future generations by inciting Americans to action. In doing so, he won a place in the hearts of many Americans, as was evidenced by those who gathered to celebrate what would have been his one-hundredth birthday. On that day in 1930, some 400 of Meeker's colleagues from around the country met in New York to recognize his work. They honored Meeker by leaving a vacant chair for him at the speakers' table. Fifty years after his death, in 1978, Congress designated the Oregon National Historic Trail, which contains 125 historic sites and 300 miles of discernible wagon ruts.

Today the Meeker Mansion in Puyallup, Washington, is open to the public. Dave and Dandy, the trusty oxen that pulled Ezra Meeker across the plains several times, were stuffed and are on exhibit in the Washington State History Museum in Tacoma, Washington. A replica of Ezra Meeker's covered wagon is also on display there, and an appointment can be made to view the original wagon, which has been stored away in a separate facility.

Right of Way

• 1996 •

1852—Eight-year-old Ellis Reynolds stood beside her father in the dark night as he toiled away. She tried to hold the tallow candle steady to illuminate his work space, yet her quiet sobbing would not allow her to be still. Though his vision was obscured, William Reynolds patiently waited for his daughter to realign the dim light. It had been an emotionally exhausting day for everyone, and the end seemed nowhere in sight.

The mid-August night had cooled to just 70 degrees and there was still work to be done before morning's light. With chisel and hammer in hand, William Reynolds pounded the hard metal of a discarded iron wagon wheel rim he had picked up en route. He was in the process of etching the memorial, "Rebecca Winters, Aged 50 Years."

In a gesture of friendship and admiration for Rebecca Winters, who was so well loved, William Reynolds planned to see to it that if her earthly remains had to be left on the forsaken prairie, at least her memory would be preserved. The Reynolds and Winters families were close friends who were journeying over the Oregon/Mormon Trail. Converts to the Mormon faith, they and 250 other believers had set out for Utah. In late June they had joined the fifty-five-wagon James C. Snow Company.

Even before they had left Kanesville, Iowa, Rebecca Winters had experienced a premonition of the outcome of their journey. During the year of preparation before their departure,

Rebecca had shared with her friends the belief that she would not live to partake of the peaceful life they hoped to attain in the Salt Lake Valley. The Winters family had already moved from Ohio to Illinois and then to Iowa to flee the anti-Mormon sentiments and religious persecution that Mormons were experiencing. Yet Rebecca was determined that she and her husband would make the 1,300-mile trip across the Trail so that her children and grandchildren could worship as they pleased.

Hiram Winters could not believe that his beloved wife of twenty-eight years, a beautiful, selfless, and faithful soul, was now gone. Her death had been devastating to all in their wagon train. Rebecca Winters had been the faithful servant to whom everyone felt comfortable confiding. Her spirit and determination had been a source of inspiration to all. The sacrifice of her life seemed unbearable. It was Rebecca's love given freely that allowed everyone to claim her as a genuine friend. Indeed, she had been the heart and soul of the caravan.

On the north side of the Platte River, some 600 miles into their journey, the dreaded cholera struck the westbound emigrants, claiming its victims one by one. Just a few short days ago, Rebecca Burdick Winters herself had been nursing her sisters back to health. Now, here on the banks of Spring Creek, Rebecca's soul had found its heavenly home. Chimney Rock was some 20 miles behind them, and the landmark of Scotts Bluff a mile or two ahead was beckoning them, but they would have to carry on without the dedicated believer and mother of five.

Hiram Winters was overwhelmed by his loss as he looked at his children, who ranged in age from eight years to twenty-seven years. He felt that he would never be able to erase from his mind their sorrowful countenances as they buried their mother.

Rebecca and Hiram had spent the better part of their lives together. They had married in 1824, converted to the Mormon faith together in 1833, and having lived worthy lives, had been "sealed" in a temple ceremony in 1846 in Nauvoo, Illinois. This special ceremony united them as husband and wife for all eternity. Rebecca therefore deserved the privilege of being buried in the sacred white temple robes, which were symbolic of purity, worthiness, and cleanliness. Instead, after the customary dressing her remains were wrapped in a quilt and were being left in the Nebraska soil.

Every attempt was made to give Rebecca a proper burial. First the men dug an exceptionally deep grave pit. At the bottom of the pit they dug a narrow trench, leaving dirt steps on either side of the trench. Rebecca's lifeless form was then lowered into the narrow trench, which would serve as the coffin. Finally, the men laid several boards across the earthen steps, thereby covering the top of the trench and creating a secure burial vault or "coffin" for Rebecca's remains. Then the earth was filled in. All male members of the Mormon faith who are properly prepared receive the priesthood, which is the authority to act as priests and lead the church. So Hiram and his sons, with divine priesthood authority, performed Rebecca's service with as much sanctity and propriety as possible out on the plains.

The final gesture of kindness that had driven William Reynolds to work tirelessly into the wee hours, chiseling away by the light of one small candle, was unveiled. The engraved iron wagon wheel rim was then pressed into an oval shape under the weight of the men and boys bearing down on the tongue of the wagon. The nearly 7-foot-long bent wheel rim was buried partway in the earth, and the grave then was filled with soil. There the iron marker would stand as a beacon to all who would pass, so that they could pay their respects to the highly revered pioneer woman. It was a tribute to the sacrifice of Rebecca's life for a greater cause, that of religious freedom for those she loved.

Following the simple service, Hiram Winters's caravan soldiered onward to the Salt Lake Valley. Rebecca's family arrived in Pleasant Grove, Utah, still deeply saddened by their loss. If only Hiram Winters had known that William Reynolds's act of compassion did indeed mark Rebecca Winters's grave for future generations, perhaps it would have brought some comfort to his broken heart.

1886–1901—In 1886 homesteaders Norman and Lorenzo DeMott found an old wagon wheel rim on their land, etched with Rebecca Winters's name. They had settled on property north of the Platte River in Scotts Bluff County, Nebraska. Realizing that the Oregon Trail passed through that area, the men fenced and protected Rebecca's grave to keep their cattle out. For more than twenty years, they tended the grave as if it had belonged to their own ancestor.

In 1899 the Chicago, Burlington, and Quincy Railroad attempted to purchase the right-of-way through the DeMotts' land to extend their rail line west through the Platte Valley along the Oregon Trail. When they learned of the grave, the railroad officials agreed to conduct a new survey so as not to disturb the site, which had become part of the Valley's heritage. Out of respect for the pioneer grave that everyone had come to know, the name *Winters* had been used to identify surroundings in the valley.

With their curiosity piqued, railroad officials attempted to further identify the occupant of the grave. They found Rebecca Winters's relatives through an ad placed in the Mormon *Deseret News* in Utah in 1901. They received thirty letters; along with a call from Rebecca's youngest son. Hyrum Winters, then sixty-nine years old, confirmed that his mother's grave was so marked and that she had died of cholera on August 15, 1852.

Though Rebecca's husband, Hiram Winters, had passed away two years earlier, all but one of their children were alive. They were surprised to learn that their mother's grave had been tended for so many years by complete strangers. The family donated the money for a proper headstone. The marker was sent to Scottsbluff, Nebraska, and placed at the grave site, which had been outlined by the railroad with a double-rail metal fence with wooden posts. The family marker was placed in front of the weatherworn iron wheel rim that read "Rebecca Winters, Aged 50 Years," which had withstood the test of time.

1920–1964—Perhaps as a testimony to her character and dedication, Rebecca Winters's grave continued to be looked after. In the 1920s a well was drilled and a hand pump installed so that employees from the railroad could tend to the grass that had been planted over the grave. Two stops on the rail line used the Winters name, and engineers blew the whistle as the train passed Rebecca's grave. Then in 1929 the Daughters of the American Revolution (D.A.R.) honored the grave site by placing a tablet there in honor of Rebecca's father, Gideon Burdick, who had served in George Washington's army.

In 1964 Rebecca Winters's grave was distinguished as a Nebraska State Historical Marker. A plaque in her honor was dedicated in a nearby park. Over the years, the park, the monument, and the grave became popular tourist attractions, attesting to Nebraska's role in the country's largest mass migration over westward trails. Finding their way to the historical marker, visitors of all ages then walked through the tall prairie grasses, sometimes using the railroad as a guide, to locate the actual grave a quarter of a mile down the track.

1995—All was well until 1995, when the Burlington Northern Railroad (BNRR), the successor to the Chicago, Burlington, and Quincy Railroad, became concerned with safety issues. The many visitors to Rebecca's grave site came within 6 feet of the rails where twenty high-speed coal trains passed daily.

Consequently, the railroad again ran an ad in the *Deseret News*. This time the ad informed Rebecca Winters's relatives that the railroad felt it was necessary to move the grave, the iron wheel rim, the family monument, and the D.A.R. stone to the park with a historical marker 900 feet away.

Though there was opposition to disturbing the peaceful resting place that had been Rebecca's for more than 143 years, the family could see that the BNRR was intent on maintaining safety. Either the grave had to be moved or a restrictive fence would be erected, denying everyone access to the grave site. A family member suggested that since the railroad had tended Rebecca's grave for so many years, perhaps it was time to help out the railroad in return.

A team of archaeologists, representatives from a local funeral home, and BNRR associates met to exhume the grave on September 5, 1995. Sixty-five of Rebecca Winters's descendants had traveled from Utah to the Nebraska prairie to attend the ceremony, too. Rebecca's descendants realized that their ancestor was important to the people of Scottsbluff, Nebraska, for over the years the Winters name had been assigned to a street, a river, a lake, two train stops, and even a voting precinct. After many hours the family saw the 6-foot-deep, 30-by-74-inch grave pit unearthed with great care.

Rebecca Winters's body had been laid out on her back, head to the West, with her left hand over her chest and her right hand over her abdomen. Carefully and respectfully the workers revealed Rebecca's skeleton, using fine brushes to remove the soil from the bones. Besides remnants of wood grains from the boards placed over the body, only two grave inclusions were identified: a small white shell button near her neck and a badly corroded piece of metal about three-quarters of an inch thick and about one inch square, found above her pelvis. The metal piece appeared to be a large belt buckle, presumably a man's, which may have been tied around Rebecca's quilted body and used to lower her form into the exceptionally deep grave. However, the archivists at the museum at Scottsbluff National Monument in Gering, Nebraska, where the metal artifact is now kept, believe that the metal was part of a lock mechanism. Perhaps it was from a memory box that contained some special mementos that were buried with Rebecca.

As the descendants, friends, railroad executives, archaeologists, and funeral directors gathered to attend to the exhumation, the workers of the Burlington Northern Railroad quietly paid their respects. Each one of the usually speeding trains that passed by slowed down to 5 miles per hour. No whistles were blown that day, but the workers showed their regard by taking off their hats and saluting Rebecca Winters.

Nearing the grave, Rebecca Winters's three-year-old great-great-great-great-granddaughter tenderly paid her respects. Upon viewing the bones, she said, "I love you, Grandma." Rebecca's 5-foot-4-inch frame was then laid in a satin-lined casket until the time of reinterment.

Bound by their common ancestral line, family members met on October 14, 1995, to give Rebecca Winters the proper burial she had long deserved. The family was uncomfortable with the modern satin-lined casket that had been chosen. A plain, old-fashioned wooden toe-pincher casket was deemed to be more appropriate for the time in which Rebecca had lived. The family chose a new Lone Star quilt with one huge star in the center—for Rebecca had been a lone star out on the prairie all these years.

Because Rebecca had been sealed in a temple ceremony 149 years earlier, her remains were finally draped with the white temple garments, and a green temple apron embroidered by a great-great-granddaughter was placed atop. With honor the great-granddaughters attended to Rebecca Winters, feeling a heightened sense of kinship as they folded the quilt over her bones. It was as if Rebecca was looking over their shoulders, giving her approval and gratitude.

Rebecca Winters's extended family had gathered to partake in her service. The oldest grandson was ninety-two years old and the youngest descendant a mere six months old. Rebecca was clearly still working through them all, bringing together those she loved.

The ceremony was officiated by Rebecca's third great-grandson, a bishop in the Mormon Church of Latter-day Saints. Rebecca's third great-granddaughter led the family in singing the hymn, "Come, Come Ye Saints," and the eulogy was given by another great-grandson.

A sixth-generation granddaughter born in 1985 and also named Rebecca Winters had visited the elder Rebecca's original grave site as a five-year-old child. At that time she had placed a small box with her Mormon "Choose the Right" ceremonial ring and a penny with the date of her birth in the dirt by the gravestone. The box had been unearthed during the exhumation and was placed in the elder Rebecca Winters's toe-pincher coffin.

Little Ellis Reynolds, who had held the candle for her father back in 1852, became one of the first female doctors in Utah. As an adult she had written a poem about Rebecca Winters. That poem was read at the service by one of Rebecca Winters's fourth great-granddaughters.

The Scottsbluff police led the large funeral procession with 125 descendants to the Rebecca Winters Memorial Park, 900 feet from the original grave site. Direct descendants of all five of Rebecca and Hiram Winters's children served as pall-bearers, along with a descendant from the Burdick family, Rebecca's ancestors.

William Reynolds's wagon wheel rim had been removed at the exhumation in September and found to be as solid as it was the day it had been installed in the ground 143 years earlier. His own great-granddaughter was there at Rebecca's reinterment to help place the oval wheel rim once again in the Nebraska soil. There it lies inside the 12-foot-by-10-foot double-railed fence with white posts. The 1929 Daughters of the American Revolution monument and the family's 1902 headstone are also there, as is the hand pump from the well. Additionally, an 8-foot-long segment of rail track lies 6 feet away, showing how close the original grave was to the BNRR line. Nearby is a historical marker that explains this remarkable saga.

1996—Rebecca Winters's family and friends gathered for a third time for the official dedication of the Rebecca Winters Memorial Park, which was deemed to be a private cemetery. On June 22, 1996, Rebecca Winters's great-grandson again paid his respects and expressed thanks to all who had helped preserve Rebecca's memory throughout the years.

In period costume, a fourth great-granddaughter, who was a fourth-grade student, presented an oral history of Rebecca's life. The sixteen-year-old Rebecca Winters had heard the legend of her namesake as a child, and she closed the ceremony with a prayer. Feeling a new connection with her ancestor, she claimed that she felt the presence of her great-great-great-great-grandmother in the gently blowing wind on that beautiful hot summer day. To her, the soft breeze that cooled everyone was Rebecca Winters's way of letting those who had gathered know that she was there.

The elder Rebecca Winters lives on as a symbol of a defender of her Mormon faith. To this day she continues to work in unifying family and friends that are descendants from her close-knit group that had traveled the Oregon Trail. In each family to which girls are born, the tradition of naming someone Rebecca helps to keep the memory of Rebecca Winters alive.

A Potpourri of Oregon Trail Facts

• The Oregon Trail traverses six states: Missouri, Kansas, Nebraska, Wyoming, Idaho, and Oregon.

• The average overland journey in a covered wagon took between four-and-a-half and five months. Today the route can be driven in four-and-a-half days or flown in four hours.

• The first emigrant to die from a firearms accident on the Oregon Trail was ironically named John Shotwell. He made the fatal mistake of getting his gun out of his wagon muzzle-first.

• Between 1840 and 1866, an estimated 500,000 emigrants headed west over the Trail.

• After crossing the Rocky Mountains and entering present-day Idaho, the emigrants in the early 1840s considered themselves officially in Oregon Territory, which extended west from the Continental Divide.

• Wagon trains lumbered over the ground at a speed of between 1 and 2 miles per hour. The emigrants walked between 10 and 15 miles per day; it took them just over one week to go a hundred miles.

• Once the emigrants left the plains and began their ascent through the mountains, the Trail became littered with treasured heirlooms and keepsakes deemed too heavy to transport any farther. This may be one reason that the officers' quarters at the military forts established along the Trail in later years seemed to be especially well-appointed.

• Four times as many emigrants traveled west in the 1850s as had in the 1840s, but the earlier excursions were found to be more worthy of newspaper coverage, so more records are available for the earlier journeys.

• There were more fatalities from accidentally discharged guns than from confrontations with Indians.

• The army sent out soldiers on the Oregon Trail as early as 1845 to retrieve individuals who were attempting to flee from their debts.

• Until 1849 a hired Trail guide was deemed to be essential to the success of a wagon train. After the trails became more defined and Trail traffic became heavier, guides were no longer considered necessary.

• Overland journeys usually began during a five-week window from the last week of April through the end of May. The starting date depended upon when the grasses on the plains were high enough to sustain the beasts of burden during the trip.

• Mass migration over the Oregon Trail by wagon was possible only after 1824, when Thomas Fitzpatrick and James Clyman identified a wide gap through the Rocky Mountains called South Pass. The gap was originally discovered in 1812.

• The greatest number of overlanders came from Missouri, Illinois, Iowa, and Indiana, and 60 percent were farmers. However, immigrants came from all over the globe to travel west on the Trail.

• The Oregon, California, and Mormon Pioneer Trails followed the general path of the Platte River for 450 miles. Between Fort Laramie, Wyoming, and Fort Bridger, Wyoming, the trails were virtually one and the same.

• Astronauts are said to be able to make out two manmade objects from space: the Great Wall of China and traces of the Oregon Trail.

• An estimated 34,000 to 45,000 lives were lost along the Oregon Trail. That averaged between 17 and 22 lives per mile.

• The nation's busiest highway, Interstate 80, follows the same path as the Oregon Trail along part of its distance, as did the Transcontinental Railroad when it was completed.

• Just 20 percent of the historic ruts created by the steady wear of wagon wheels along the Oregon Trail remain identifiable today.

• Outfitting a family of four, including wagon, animals, and provisions cost between $500 and $1,000. In today's dollars that would be between $7,986 and $15,972. Emigrants often had to save their wages for one to three years to afford the trip.

• There are approximately 200 known graves, most unmarked, along the Oregon Trail. To prevent the graves of their loved ones from being disinterred by grave robbers or animals, emigrants often buried the dead directly under the path of the Trail. Wagons passing over helped to obliterate any sign so the graves could not be detected.

• It is estimated that one out of every 250 emigrants kept a diary or journal while heading west. In later years some emigrants wrote down their reminiscences, adding to the history of overland travel.

• The first third of the Oregon Trail was geographically the easiest, but it was also the most disease-ridden. The terrain of the last third of the Trail was the most physically challenging.

• Between 1841 and 1869, the heyday of the Oregon Trail, there were nine U.S. presidents.

• The completion of the Transcontinental Railroad in 1869 is said to have brought an end to the wagon-train era. However, as late as 1895 covered wagons could still be seen heading west.

• By 1899 all Native American tribes in Oregon were on government-designated reservations.

• A few emigrants en route had quite the surprise when they climbed trees to view what they thought were eagles' nests. It was the custom of some Indian tribes to place their dead in scaffolds built in the tree branches so that the deceased would be closer to the spirit world.

• Oregon joined the Union as the thirty-third state on February 14, 1859. Today it is the ninth-largest state in area.

• Some historians consider the end of the Oregon Trail to have been The Dalles, a place of rocky rapids along the Columbia River. Others feel that since most emigrants were headed for the Willamette Valley, they still had to either raft down the Columbia River or scale the Cascade Mountains to reach their final destination.

• The first place in which the Oregon Trail split was at the "Parting of the Ways" in south-central Wyoming. The left fork headed to Utah and California, and the right fork was the Sublette Cutoff, which headed to Oregon.

• The second place where the Oregon Trail split was just past Soda Springs, Idaho. The left fork took the Hudspeth Cutoff heading to California, and the right fork continued on to Oregon.

• During wind and rainstorms, the wheels of the covered wagons were anchored to stakes driven into the ground and attached with ox chains so the wagons wouldn't blow over.

• In 1978, Congress designated the 2,000-mile Trail as the National Historic Oregon Trail.

Where to Visit the Oregon Trail

Chimney Rock
Chimney Rock Visitor Center
Chimney Rock Road
Bayard, NE 69336
(308) 586–2581
chimrock@scottsbluff.net
www.nps.gov/chro/

Craters of the Moon National Monument
P.O. Box 29
Arco, ID 83213
(208) 527–3257
www.nps.gov/crmo/
www.idahohistory.net/OTcraters.html

The Dalles, Oregon
www.ohwy.com/or/t/thedalle.htm
www.el.com/to/thedalles/

Deschutes Historical Center
Wall and Idaho
129 NW Idaho Street
Bend, OR 97701
(541) 389–1813
http://deschutes.historical.museum

Donner Memorial State Park and Emigrant Trail Museum
12593 Donner Pass Road
Truckee, CA 96161
(530) 582–7892
www.americansouthwest.net/california/donner_memorial/state_park.html

Ezra Meeker Historical Society/Meeker Mansion
312 Spring Street
P.O. Box 103
Puyallup, WA 98371
(253) 848–1770
www.meekermansion.org/main.html

Independence Rock
Highway 220, 50 miles west of Casper, WY
(307) 577–5150
wyoshpo.state.wy.us/indrock2.htm
wyoparks.state.wy.us/irock1.htm

Lewelling Quaker Shrine
401 South Main
Salem, IA 52649
(319) 385–2460
www.henrycountytourism.org

National Frontier Trails Center
318 West Pacific Street
Independence, MO 64050
(816) 325–7575
www.frontiertrailsmuseum.org

The National Historic Oregon Trail Interpretive Center
P.O. Box 987
Baker City, OR 97811
(541) 523–1843
oregontrail.blm.gov/

The National Oregon/California Trail Center
P.O. Box 323
Montpelier, ID 83254
(866) 847–3800
www.oregontrailcenter.org

Rebecca Winters's Grave Site
Scottsbluff, NE
www.geocities.com/Heartland/Plains/8019/nerw.html

Scotts Bluff National Monument
Oregon Trail Museum and Visitor Center
P.O. Box 27
Gering, NE 69341–0027
(308) 436–4340
scottsbluff.areaparks.com/
www.nps.gov/scbl

Soda Springs, ID
Soda Springs Chamber of Commerce
P.O. Box 697
Soda Springs, ID 83276
(208) 547–4964
(888) 399–0888
www.sodaspringsid.com
www.idahohistory.net/OTsprings.html

Solomon Butcher's photographs
www.nebraskahistory.org

Thousand Springs, Idaho
Caribou and Thousand Springs Scenic Byways
www.idahorec.org/PDF/OregonTrail.pdf
http://www.pbs.org/idahoportrait/tour/thousandtour.html

Bibliography

Books

Applegate, Jesse A. *Recollections of My Boyhood.* Fairfield, WA: Ye Galleon Press, 1934.

Applegate, Jesse. *A Day with the Cow Column in 1843.* Fairfield, WA: Ye Galleon Press, 1934.

Belshaw, Maria Parsons. *Crossing the Plains to Oregon in 1853.* Fairfield, WA: Ye Galleon Press, 2000.

Bial, Raymond. *Lifeways—The Sioux.* New York: Benchmark Books, 2001.

Blackwood, Gary L. *Life on the Oregon Trail.* San Diego, CA: Lucent Books, 1999.

Bleeker, Sonia. *The Sioux Indians: Hunters and Warriors of the Plains.* New York: William Morrow and Company, 1962.

Brown, Randy, and Reg Duffin. *Graves and Sites on the Oregon and California Trails.* Independence, MO: Oregon–California Trails Association, 1998.

Calabro, Marion. *The Perilous Journey of the Donner Party.* New York: Clarion Books, 1999.

Clark, Roland K., and Lowell Tiller. *Terrible Trail: The Meek Cutoff, 1845.* Caldwell, ID: Caxton Printers, 1966.

Conrad, Pam. *Prairie Visions: The Life and Times of Solomon Butcher.* New York: HarperCollins, 1991.

Delano, Alonzo. *Across the Plains and Among the Diggings.* New York: Wilson–Erickson, Inc., 1854, 1936.

Douthit, Mary Osborn, ed. *The Souvenir of Western Women.* Portland, OR: Anderson & Duniway Company, 1905.

Duniway, Abigail Scott. *Captain Gray's Company or Crossing the Plains and Living in Oregon.* Portland, OR: S. J. McCormick, 1859.

Faragher, John Mack. *Women and Men on the Overland Trail.* New Haven, CT: Yale University Press, 1979.

Franzwa, Gregory M. *The Oregon Trail Revisited.* St. Louis, MO: Patrice Press, Inc., 1972.

Freedman, Russell. *Children of the Wild West.* New York: Clarion Books, 1983.

Greenberg, Judith E., and Helen Carey McKeever. *A Pioneer Woman's Memoir: Based on the Journal of Arabella Clemens Fulton.* New York: Franklin Watts, 1995.

Haines, Aubrey L. *Historic Sites Along the Oregon Trail.* Gerald, MO: Patrice Press, Inc., 1981.

Handsaker, Uncle Sam. *Pioneer Life.* Eugene, OR: Sam Handsaker, 1908.

Hargrove, Jim. *America the Beautiful—Nebraska.* Chicago: Children's Press, 1989.

Hastings, Lansford W. *The Emigrants' Guide to Oregon and California, Containing Scenes and Incidents of a Party of Oregon Emigrants.* Bedford, MA: Applewood Books, 1994 (originally published in 1845).

Hewitt, James. *Eye-Witnesses to Wagon Trains West.* New York: Charles Scribner's Sons, 1973.

Hirsch, E. D. Jr., Joseph F. Kett, and James Trefil. *The Dictionary of Cultural Literacy.* Boston: Houghton Mifflin, 1988.

Hofsinde, Robert (Gray-Wolf). *Indian Costumes.* New York: William Morrow and Co., 1968.

Holmes, Kenneth L. *Covered Wagon Women: Diaries and Letters from the Western Trails, 1840–1890.* Glendale, CA: Arthur H. Clark Company, 1983.

Hoover, Herbert T. *Indians of North America: The Yankton Sioux.* New York: Chelsea House Publishers, 1988.

Ito, Tom. *World History Series: The California Gold Rush.* San Diego, CA: Lucent Books, 1997.

Kallen, Stuart A. *Native American Chiefs and Warriors.* San Diego, CA: Lucent Books, 1999.

Kallen, Stuart A. *The Way People Live/Life on the American Frontier.* San Diego, CA: Lucent Books, 1999.

Kimball, Violet T. *Stories of Young Pioneers in Their Own Words.* Missoula, MT: Mountain Press Publishing Co., 2000.

Lampman, Evelyn Sibley. *Tree Wagon.* Garden City, NY: Junior Literary Guild, 1953.

Lipman, Jean. *Rufus Porter Rediscovered.* New York: Clarkson N. Potter, Inc., 1980.

Lipman, Jean. *Rufus Porter, Yankee Pioneer.* New York: Clarkson N. Potter, Inc., 1968.

Lockley, Fred, and Mike Helm, eds. *Conversations with Pioneer Women: The Lockley Files.* Eugene, OR: Rainy Day Press, 1981.

Mattes, Merrill J. *The Great Platte River Road.* Lincoln: Nebraska State Historical Society, 1969.

Mattes, Merrill J. *Platte River Road Narratives: A Descriptive Bibliography of Travel over the Great Central Overland Route to Oregon, California, Utah, Colorado, Montana, and Other Western States and Territories.* Urbana, IL: University of Illinois Press, 1988.

Meeker, Ezra. *The Ox Team, or The Old Oregon Trail.* New York: Ezra Meeker., 1906. / Mt. Vernon, IN: Windmill Publications, 2000.

Murphy, Virginia Reed. *Across the Plains in the Donner Party.* Edited by Karen Zeinert. North Haven, CT: Linnet Books, 1996.

Newell, Olive. *Tail of the Elephant.* Cedar Ridge, CA: Nevada County Historical Society, 1997.

Olsen, Beth Radmall. *Among the Remnant Who Lingered: The History of Rebecca Burdick and Hiram Winters and Their Families.* Orem, UT: Micro Dynamics Electronic Publishing, Inc., 1997.

Parkman, Francis, Jr. *The Oregon Trail: Sketches of Prairie and Rocky-Mountain Life.* Williamston, MA: Corner House, 1980.

Place, Marion T. *Westward on the Oregon Trail.* New York: American Heritage, 1962.

Porter, A. P. *Nebraska.* Minneapolis, MN: Lerner Publications, 1991.

Schlissel, Lillian. *Women's Diaries of the Westward Journey.* New York: Schocken Books, 1982, 1992.

Sherrow, Victoria. *Life During the Gold Rush (The Way People Live).* San Diego, CA: Lucent Books, 1998.

Sirvaitis, Karen. *Utah.* Minneapolis, MN: Lerner Publications, 1991.

Steedman, Scott. *Inside Story—A Frontier Fort on the Oregon Trail.* Illustrated by Mark Bergin. New York: Peter Bedrick Books, 1994.

Stefoff, Rebecca. *Children of the Westward Trail.* Brookfield, CT: Millbrook Press, 1996.

Stone, Bev, and Gary Stone. *Stone by Stone on the Oregon Trail.* Kimberly, ID: Bridgetown Printing Co., 1993.

True, Charles Frederick, and Carro True. *The Overland Memoir of Charles Frederick True.* Edited by Sally Ralston True. Independence, MO: Oregon–California Trails Association, 1993.

Unruh, John D. Jr. *The Plains Across: The Overland Emigrants and the Trans-Mississippi West, 1840–1860.* Urbana, IL: University of Illinois Press, 1979.

Webber, Bert. *Comprehensive Index to Oregon Trail Diaries.* Medford, OR: Webb Research Group, 1991.

Webber, Bert. *The Oregon and California Trail Diary of Jane Gould in 1862.* Eugene, OR: Webb Research Group, 1987.

Webber, Bert. *The Oregon Trail Diary of Twin Sisters, Cecilia Adams and Parthenia Blank in 1852.* Eugene, OR: Webb Research Group, 1990.

Zeman, Anne, and Kate Kelly. *Everything You Need to Know About American History.* New York: Scholastic, Inc., 1994.

Interviews

Benion, Perry, interview by Tricia Martineau Wagner, January 8, 2003.

Clause, Vickie, interviews by Tricia Martineau Wagner, November 2002–January 2003.

Cooke, John, interview by Tricia Martineau Wagner, February 1, 2002.

DeMott, Norman, interview by Tricia Martineau Wagner, January 4, 2003.

Freeman, Dee and Norman, interview by Tricia Martineau Wagner, January 1, 2003.

Greathouse, Roma Jean, interview by Tricia Martineau Wagner, January 7, 2003.

Harrison, Allen, interview by Tricia Martineau Wagner, March 12, 2002.

Howard, Gordon, interview by Tricia Martineau Wagner, October 10, 2001.

Howard, Kevin, interview by Tricia Martineau Wagner, October 10, 2001.

Johnson, Art, interview by Tricia Martineau Wagner, October 10, 2001.

Klutts, Charlie, interview by Tricia Martineau Wagner, December 12, 2002.

Knowles, Beth, interview by Tricia Martineau Wagner, January 2003.

Knutsen, Dean, interview by Tricia Martineau Wagner, October 10, 2001.

Kramer, Dennis, interview by Tricia Martineau Wagner, December 2002.

Olsen, Beth, interviews by Tricia Martineau Wagner, November 2002–January 2003.

Steinacher, Terry, interview by Tricia Martineau Wagner, January 2003.

Tingey, Rebecca Winters, interview by Tricia Martineau Wagner, January 7, 2003.

Tucker, Carol, interview by Tricia Martineau Wagner, January 7, 2003.

Winters, Anika, interview by Tricia Martineau Wagner, December 18, 2002.

Winters, Dean, interview by Tricia Martineau Wagner, January 2003.

Winters, Gerry and Alden, interviews by Tricia Martineau Wagner, January 8–11, 2003.

Winters, Rebecca, interview by Tricia Martineau Wagner, January 8, 2003.

Winters, Rebecca Bennett, interviews by Tricia Martineau Wagner, January 8–11, 2003.

Winters, Que, interview by Tricia Martineau Wagner, January 2003.

Magazines

"Cowboys, Indians, and Pioneers." *Southeast Idaho Travel Guide.* September 2001.

Duffin, Reg P., "The Miller–Tate Murder and the John F. Miller Grave," *Overland Journal,* Fall 1987.

Ellison, Joseph W., "The Beginnings of the Apple Industry in Oregon," *Agricultural History,* October 1937, 11:322–343.

"Great Vacation Drives," *U.S. News & World Report,* September 1998.

"History of Agriculture, Father of Horticulture on the Pacific Coast, the Lewelling Family," *The American Fruit Growers Magazine,* August 1947.

Munkres, Robert L. "Crime on the Trail." *Overland Journal,* Fall, 1994.

"The Oldest Pioneer," *American History,* August 2001.

"Trails West," *National Geographic,* 1979.

"With Settlement, the Land Blossomed . . .", *The Sou'wester,* Spring 1966.

Newspapers

Burnes, Brian, "Ox Yokes Lift Slavery's Chains." *Kansas City Star,* February 5, 1994.

Haight, Frank J., "Young School Bears Name of Former Slave." *Examiner,* May 2, 1986.

Harris, Doug, "Burlington Northern to Move Rebecca Winter's Grave Site," *Gering Courier,* August 24, 1995.

Harris, Doug, "Rebecca Winters Re-interred at Family and Public Services." *Gering Courier,* October 19, 1995.

Harris, Doug, "The Grave," *Gering Courier,* October 19, 1995.

Hendricks, Mike, "Ex-Slave Was a Success in Early Independence," *Kansas City Star,* February 23, 1986.

Kinnaird, Clark, "Your America," *Oregonian Newspaper,* Portland, April 17, 1965.

O'Brien, Patrick, "Hiram Young: The Free Black in Antebellum and Reconstruction Missouri: 1850–1880," *Jackson County Historical Society,* January–June 1984.

"The Oregon Trail," *Idaho State Journal,* April 29, 2001.

Stephens, Tammy, "The National Oregon/California Trail Center, Second Annual Legacy Edition," *News-Examiner,* Summer 2000.

Swanson, Kim, and Rick Meyers, "Ancestor Unearthed," *Star–Herald,* September 6, 1995.

Troyer, Dianna, "Montpelier Center Revives Oregon Trail," *American Profile, August 12–18, 2001.*

Other Sources

"The Lewelling Quaker House," Lewelling Quaker Shrine Brochure, Salem, IA, 2001.

"Luelling, Henderson," *Dictionary of American Biography,* New York: Henry County Tourism Association, 1993.

"Mormon Trail Sites in the Casper, Wyoming Area." Casper, Wyoming, Stake of the Church of Jesus Christ of Latter-day Saints, 1997

Notes from a brown folder given to Mrs. H. J. Lewelling by Jane Lewelling.

Olsen, Beth R., "Death on the Plains in 1852 Made Rebecca Winters Legendary," September 1995.

Oregon State Archives. Oregon State Library.

Rebecca Winters Scrapbooks, North Platte Valley Gering Museum.

"The Rebecca Winters Story," Scotts Bluff National Monument Brochure.

"Soda Springs, Idaho . . . Historic Oregon Trail Oasis." Idaho Travel Council Brochure.

Steinacher, Terry L.,"Report on the Exhumation of the Rebecca Winters Grave Site, Scotts Bluff County, Nebraska," Nebraska State Historic Preservation Office, September 11, 1995.

"Welcome to Independence Rock, the Register of the Desert." Casper Area Convention and Visitor Bureau Brochure.

Media

The National Oregon/California Trail Center at Clover Creek, video, 2001.

The Oregon Trail, CD, National Historic Oregon Trail Interpretive Center, 1997.

Munkres, Dr. Robert L., *Trail Facts*, http://calcite.rocky.edu/octa/facts.htm

http://bluebook.state.or.us/notable/notwhite.htm

http://calcite.rocky.edu/octa/soda.htm

http://geocities.com/orgone_2000/oregontrailthird.html

www.isu.edu/~trinmich/IndyRock.html

www.nebraskahistory.org

www.nps.gov/mopi/mopi.htm

Index

About the Author

Tricia Martineau Wagner, an Ohio native, is an experienced elementary school teacher and reading specialist. When she moved to the San Francisco Bay area, Tricia became intrigued with the westward migration of the pioneers over the Oregon Trail. This is her first book for TwoDot Books, an imprint of the Globe Pequot Press. Tricia now makes her home in Charlotte, North Carolina, with her husband, Mark, and their children, Kelsey and Mitch.